THE ELEPHANT'S DILEMMA

THE
ELEPHANT'S DILEMMA

BREAK FREE AND REIMAGINE YOUR FUTURE AT WORK

JON BOSTOCK

LIONCREST
PUBLISHING

THE ELEPHANT'S DILEMMA

Break Free and Reimagine Your Future at Work

ISBN   978-1-5445-0985-3 *Hardcover*
   978-1-5445-0984-6 *Paperback*
   978-1-5445-0983-9 *Ebook*

To Evan and Will,

I hope this inspires you and others to make the world a better place.

Love, Dad

CONTENTS

INTRODUCTION

My job was a joke—a literal joke. Did you ever see the TV sitcom *30 Rock*? The show's creators decided the funniest, most ridiculous job for the goofy character played by Alec Baldwin was that of Vice President of East Coast Television and Microwave Oven Programming for General Electric. In real life, I led GE's microwave oven product line. However, without the television department under my belt, the job was not as funny as Alec Baldwin would have you believe.

Instead of running around a TV set making quick-witted banter with Tina Fey, I sat at my faux wood desk on the second floor of Building Four, the gem of GE's sprawling, cockroach-infested Consumer and Industrial Campus in Louisville, Kentucky. From the air, the campus looked like semi-conductor chips on a green board. On a particularly gray Tuesday, I was reading the Robert Wood Johnson Foundation's *State of Obesity: Better Policies for a Healthier America* report. This was back in 2010, and obesity rates in the United States had been climbing for decades. As I was leading a product line that revolved around cooking, I wanted to understand the macro trends impacting diets and cooking behaviors, and I was curious about the report's findings.

As I studied the depressing report, I was hit by the extent of the obesity problem. So many people were eating unhealthily and becoming dangerously overweight that the report called it an epidemic. Then, I saw the kicker: The report called out microwave ovens for contributing to the issue. *Oh, fuck*, I thought. *Microwaves are my life, and they're terrible for everyone. Awesome.* If this were *30 Rock*, the irony would make you laugh, but I wasn't laughing.

Of course, fast food, busy lifestyles, and other issues were cited as influencing factors, but I wasn't spending my every working hour on those things. I was dedicated to the mighty microwave, which was now officially charged with having a negative impact on our country.

In my own home, we barely used the microwave. I realize that's not a great advertisement for the product, but my wife and I enjoyed cooking. We occasionally used the microwave to reheat leftovers, but we mostly relied on the stove and oven to cook meals from scratch. Now, we have kids who love microwave popcorn, but back then, I hadn't discovered the joy of pre-buttered popcorn kernels.

The report said that microwaves made it easier for people to eat unhealthy food. Even though that wasn't my experience, I knew it was true. At GE, we'd designed our microwaves with convenience buttons to easily cook pizza, hot pockets, and, of course, butter-smothered microwave popcorn, amongst other unhealthy snacks. There was no button for cooking kale.

As I sat there flipping through the pages of the report, it dawned on me that I could influence this thing that was negatively impacting others. I didn't have to be the big, bad microwave manager. Instead, I could help change this story. I was in a position to make the microwave a tool for good instead of an instrument of obesity. This wasn't just an option; it felt like a responsibility I was charged with figuring out. As a leader in the exciting world of microwaving, I could observe trends and incorporate those trends into my day-to-day work. This was my first leadership role, and I was finally empowered to make real, influential changes to my product line. Sure, I wasn't selling a range of cancer-curing drugs, but according to this report, microwaves had an impact on consumer health. And I wanted that impact to be for good.

Let's be honest here: I also wanted to make money. I wasn't going to keep my glamorous job as a microwave oven product line leader if I didn't meet our profit projections. But there are a lot of ways to make money, right? I wanted to do it in a way that created a positive impact on the world. It just felt like the right thing to do.

THE ELEPHANT'S DILEMMA

This was the first time I considered the elephant's dilemma. I didn't know that phrase back then, but it refers to a creature that doesn't know its own strength. Imagine an elephant at one of those old-school circuses with a high-top tent, trapeze artists, the world's hairiest man, and PETA-offenses galore. At a very early age, even before they teach it to jump through hoops, the elephant is tied up with a heavy chain around its leg. It's held back and can't roam free.

As the elephant grows, it doesn't need a stronger chain to keep it restrained; it learned that it couldn't get away, so it stopped trying. Now, a small rope around its leg keeps the elephant in place, and the poor creature has no idea that it could easily break free if it were willing to try. Elephants are one of the strongest and most surprisingly agile animals in the world. They're smart. They never forget. They remember their mama and their home and their family. They're pretty magical creatures. But when elephants are held back as babies, they grow into big, powerful adults who still believe they're held back.

At GE, I was held back without even realizing it. I was kept in place by the constraints of the business world I'd grown up in—the world most of us are raised in, regardless of where we work. I saw how my category was run, how business was performed, and I tethered myself to that. When I read the obesity report, I considered for the first time that I could break free from the same-old, same-old pattern of producing and selling microwaves that help people eat junk more easily. I began to consider that *perhaps* I was strong enough to break free of that restraint.

TUGGING THE CHAIN

I went to my team and proposed that we focus on marketing microwaves as a way of preparing healthy food. I wanted to make microwaves work for a healthy lifestyle. There was some natural skepticism, as there often is when you propose a change in a large company. The leaders above me had just one question: Will this new direction make us money? Yes or no? Yes, I said.

Then, I had to articulate why that was true. There was a valid market segment looking for tools to help them with a healthier lifestyle. There were government and public health initiatives already underway to promote healthy eating, and these were opportunities for partnership. We could work with the Let's Move! campaign led by Michelle Obama and the MyPlate program from the USDA Center for Nutrition Policy and Promotion to tell the story that healthy eating can be easier than many people believe.

Plus, taking no action would mean we could be perceived as part of the obesity epidemic, which could actually lead to a sales loss.

I got buy-in from the leadership, and we created a convenience menu system tied to healthy foods. That meant our new microwaves had easy buttons to cook grains and vegetables. We provided cooking menus showing people how easy it was to prepare, say, broccoli in their new microwave. We partnered with a retailer to get the product on the shelf.

And, well, I'd love to say we reduced obesity by 30 percent. We single-handedly cured an epidemic at the press of a microwave button! Not really. In truth, I don't know the outcome. Awareness of the MyPlate and Let's Move! initiatives undoubtedly had a positive effect. Our product sold well. I have no data on obesity rates and microwaves, though, and you just have to look around to see that obesity is still an issue. However, in a sea of sameness where every damn microwave looks and functions the same as at the dawn of microwaving, I think we made a good decision. It wasn't exactly disruptive—in fact, it was kind of goofy—but it was a shift in the right direction.

Importantly for me, it was a tug on the chain that I believed was around my ankle. It was my first step toward breaking free from the way business was always done. It allowed me to reimagine what was possible at work.

ELEPHANTS AT WORK

If you're like me, you're an elephant at work. When you were younger, you entered the workplace and couldn't even fathom the opportunity ahead of you. You showed up at your desk every day, worked hard, and played your part in the big, bureaucratic machine of corporate America. Decades later, you've become pretty big in your area, but you've remained chained to the rhythm of every day. You sit in front of a computer screen, run through the motions, fixate on the next quarter's goals, scroll Facebook, and watch the world grow up around you. One day, you see an old college friend whose kid just graduated, or your niece turns eighteen, or your mentor passes away, and you realize life is slipping by while you're stuck with your head down, oblivious to the days ticking past. You're lost in the moment. You feel unfulfilled. You're wondering if this job is all there is.

But you're also strong. Powerful. Able to break free from boring business and create a more fulfilling existence. You have the potential to reimagine your future in the workplace. You can pull free from the chains of "how things are done" and find ways to make your future work more meaningful—even if it's just by redesigning goofy microwave menus.

When you break free of the old constraints, you can also put your future to work *for you*. You can create a future that works for your benefit, and which positively affects those you love. You can even put that idea on steroids and affect the future of the broader world in which you live. You can do work that significantly improves the lives of your kids and their kids and their kids after them. You can work to leave a positive legacy in and for the world.

LOOKING BACK

Most of us needn't look far back to see examples of people who broke free of the constraints they were born into so they could leave a legacy for the future. I'm an American with immigrant ancestors. Both my parents were born in the States, but their parents were not. My paternal grandmother was from Belarus. When her country became unsafe, she traveled through Russia and Japan to the US with a lot of luck and a lot of help. There were only about two thousand Jews who survived that passage, and she was among them. My mother's side is also Jewish, and my maternal grandparents fled their homeland to find safety in the US. Within a year of arriving, my grandmother gave birth to my mom and passed away. My grandfather raised his baby daughter, and later his grandkids—me and my brother, with immense help from those around him.

Although my grandparents came from different places and lived separate lives, they all escaped difficult circumstances to create a better future for themselves and their kids. They left their country, their religion, their possessions, and extended family members. They struggled. They broke free from the chains tying them to their homeland and embarked on a journey to do something meaningful for their future.

As Americans, many of us share similar ancestral histories. You might need to look back a few more generations to see these stories. Or not. Either way, it's inspiring to see how our ancestors broke free and reimagined a better future for themselves and their families.

LEAPING FORWARD

Thanks to the leaps my ancestors took, my life has been pretty stable. I didn't have much growing up, but I've had a successful career. And most of that success came because I was inspired by my ancestors to break free of my circumstances and take big leaps.

The microwave thing was kind of silly, but it was a life-changing step. It taught me that I could take macro trends and use them to reimagine my work. With that attitude, I became the general manager of consumer ventures and joined GE's business innovations group led by Beth Comstock. We worked on trademark licensing initiatives, which sounds boring, but we got to reimagine GE's marketing and innovation efforts.

Eventually, I decided I wanted to make a more significant impact. I wanted to contribute to creating more environmentally sustainable companies. So, I leaped into a small company called Big Ass Fans, which made, you guessed it, large industrial and commercial ceiling fans.

The company was trying to transition from a founder-led setup to a more sustainable structure that would see it through the next one hundred years or so, since the founder was unlikely to live that long. It was a fast-moving, fun-as-hell place where I got to make a positive impact. That impact turned out to be negotiating the business's sale to a company that could look after it long after the founder was gone.

After the sale, I took an even bigger step and, with my business partner, launched Truman's, a non-toxic cleaning products company. We saw this $10 billion-dollar spray cleaner market, where big companies pay a fortune to ship a gazillion bottles filled with 98 percent water, then pass those costs onto customers, and thought, *We can do better than that, for consumers and the planet.*

In 2019, we launched as a direct-to-consumer cleaning subscription business with just four products covering the entire home—and they're all concentrates that users dilute themselves. There's no shipping of unnecessary water. No ridiculous color additives and chemical "sunshine meadow" scents. Everything is non-toxic, conveniently delivered, easy-to-use, and better for the planet.

Just months after our launch, Fast Company honored Truman's as a "World Changing Idea." We've since won a bunch of awards, received $5 million in investment funding from a massive brand, and drawn worldwide attention to toxicity in the home. And to top it off, I'm actually having fun at work. I finally feel like I'm doing something *really* useful, not just "microwave menu useful," and that's helped me relax and sink into the work. It took many years, many steps, and many missteps, but I finally broke free from a good-on-paper yet boring-as-hell career. I discovered my strength and founded a fun, fulfilling business that's creating a more sustainable future, both for my career and for the environment in which my kids will grow up.

IT STARTS WITH MOVEMENT

This book will show you how to break free from the constraints of business and reimagine your future at work. It'll show you how to make business decisions that are more sustainable, more radical, and more disruptive so that you can leap into a more fulfilling future. I'm not saying you must take careless risks. I mean that the antidote to being stuck in a career rut is *to move*. If you feel like you're not doing anything significant with your life, you need to start *doing things*. Moving. Leaping forward.

You can do anything you want. You can look up from the day-to-day grind and look further ahead than the next quarter's profit projections. If our ancestors can leap into a new life in a new country, you can shift out of your rut and into a more fulfilling, meaningful career that will make your future work for you.

We're not going to do this through "five simple steps to a fun new job." This book isn't about following a prescribed process to a predetermined result. No, this is a battle cry. It's a call to arms. In these pages, I'll ask you to stand up, assess your life, and drive sustainable innovation within your world.

And when I say "sustainable," I'm not talking about saving all the whales or cutting plastic consumption—unless that's what gets you going. I'm referring to actions you can sustain because they work really well. I'm talking about having a true competitive advantage because you can keep your company or division or startup going regardless of the way the world changes. I want you to contribute to your future and the world in a way that lasts into your legacy. That's sustainability in business.

This book will show you how to break free and create an innovative business with a true competitive advantage. You'll see why this isn't just a nice idea but a real necessity. You'll learn the three main paths to take impactful business

leaps: reimagining products and services, redesigning operations and supply chains, and aligning organizations into
radical sustainability. You'll learn how these elements can
elicit change in isolation or be combined for greater effect.
You'll also get tools to support your efforts, so the risk of
breaking free feels less, well, risky. You'll learn how all this
will make your work and the world infinitely better, leaving
you more fulfilled than you imagine possible.

So, let's go, elephant. Let's imagine your future at work.
And you know the first step to looking forward? You have
to lift your eyes and look beyond your living room.

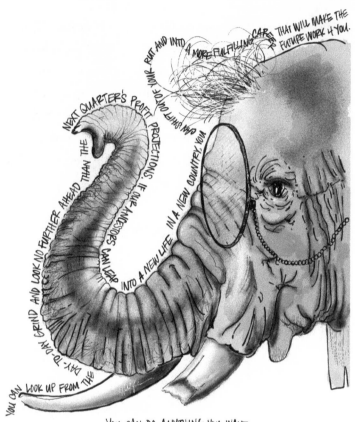

YOU CAN DO ANYTHING YOU WANT.

CHAPTER ONE

THE VIEW FROM THE BUBBLE

"The McNeighborhood" is a nickname given to those sprawling suburban areas built across North America a few decades ago. All the houses look virtually the same. You'd waltz into a showroom office, choose one of the four deluxe floorplans available for new-build houses in that area, and order your dream home—as easy as ordering from McDonald's. You'd move into your McMansion with a double garage—because, of course, nothing in the suburbs is in walkable distance—and live comfortably.

For many people, a McMansion is the epitome of the American dream. It represents safety and comfort. And why not get a nice, big house when you can afford it? People live in these places because they want a safe space for their family—and that's a noble desire. It's what I want for my family. However, when our family moved to New Orleans, it was important to my wife and me that we found a nice, safe home *outside* of a McNeighborhood. We choose an urban area so we could avoid the not-so-awesome side effect of living in suburbia: the isolation.

When the novel coronavirus forced the world to shelter-in-place, we all felt how crazy-making isolation could be. But even without those extraordinary restrictions, sprawling suburban areas can feel isolating. That sounds weird, given these are communities of houses upon houses crammed together between highways. But they're markedly different to cities. Cities were designed to bring people together. They were constructed for residents to live, work, and play in a common area. They encourage people to walk around, see their neighbors, and engage with their surroundings.

For those who live in a McNeighborhood, they're a thirty-minute drive from the downtown office (on a good day). It's a twenty-minute drive to the nearest Costco. The closest store is probably a gas station at the entrance to the community. Some people walk their dogs, but most go from the office to the car, then straight into the house.

I know I sound like I'm down on suburbia, but that's not the real problem here. The issue is that these neighborhoods encourage people to live in a bubble. They reduce a person's connection to their community. The McNeighborhood is an illustration; there are certainly other situations that encourage people to live an insular life, caring only about what's inside their bubble. Whatever the cause and whatever the redeeming factors (because I know there *are* great things about those lifestyles), we can't ignore the effects of isolation.

When you live in a bubble, surrounded by a world that looks the same in every direction, you become oblivious to the outside world. When your community is packed with the same houses, same yards, same SUVs in the driveway, with nothing unique or interesting, it doesn't engage your mind. You get used to all the conformity, all the sameness, and you look elsewhere for something interesting. You turn your attention inward to your individual family unit.

THE ISSUE WITH LOOKING INWARD

Of course, I'm not suggesting it's a bad thing to pay attention to your family. I like my family. I like hanging out with them. But let's look at what happens when you *only* focus on what's inside your bubble. Imagine a family with a dual income; the woman is, let's say, a lawyer making a good salary. The man's a doctor. Between them, they've saved a decent financial buffer. They can afford great vacations. They have tuition money for their kids' educations. They think, *We've got this life stuff figured out. There's food on our table. The future's secure. Our kids will be okay.* But is that sense of security justified?

Those parents believe they've set their children up for success, but as those kids grow up, they won't live in the same bubble. At some point, they'll leave Mom and Dad's house and head into the wide world. Those parents are assuming that the world will have clean waterways. They believe the air will be clean and food systems functional. I hate to be a downer, but I don't share those assumptions.

The US generally appears to have stabilized. Compare the state of our society today to the developments of our past. At one time, there was a tremendous amount of progress in our country. We built the railroad and highway systems. We put electricity in every home. We made it to the moon, and we flooded the country with internet access. Then, progress slowed. We stabilized. We stopped taking moon shots and, instead, focused on less weighty, less impactful innovations. We stopped coming together to take giant swings that shook our culture and became more divided. Innovation started coming from smaller private and commercial efforts that didn't have the same cultural impact. I mean, can you think of an innovation in the last twenty years that was as impactful as building the interstate highway network? Can you recall a recent innovation that brought people together in the same way we gathered to watch the moon landing? No. The world continues to innovate, but in small, more divided, less impactful ways.

If we don't start to innovate in ways more reminiscent of our past, we'll remain flat while the world's challenges peak. If we keep operating the same way we are today, with small steps taken here and there but no massive cultural swings, we'll end up with a lot of problems. Pollution, cleanliness, food systems, waterways, airways, and the atmosphere will deteriorate because we won't innovate fast enough to keep up with their challenges. Even issues like gun violence, mental health, and homelessness will rise if we don't actively seek to combat them. The solutions we have in place today will not hold up to the challenges of tomorrow. And often, we don't correctly predict what those challenges will be. Most of us did not see, or at least take seriously, the threat of a pandemic. I sure as hell wasn't ready for the impact the novel coronavirus had on the world. Simply put, if we don't innovate, the world will not be a better place for our kids—and no college fund or stable upbringing will protect them from that.

It's not enough to sit in your bubble and think, *Oh, the world is great. In our little life, everything is fine.* In fifty years, if gun violence has spread throughout cities, if there are more pandemics and massive health issues, if only 10 percent of the population has access to clean water, this is going to impact everyone's bubble. Even if *your* kids still have access to resources, that's not okay. We need better for our world. If terrible diseases are rampant and life expectancy plummets, that's not good for anyone. Even those who are somewhat protected cannot continue to thrive when surrounded by enormous amounts of shittiness. It's not sustainable for one in ten people to benefit from the world's resources. That percentage won't last. It'll drop to 8 percent, then 6, then 2, and then it will go away and we'll all be screwed.

I know—I'm an absolute fountain of positivity. You should see me on a rant after a glass of wine. I'm a hoot as a dinner party guest. But there's a good reason I'm laying this on thick. We need to acknowledge that those of us sitting in nice, safe, comfortable bubbles are probably best positioned to create positive change. And we do need change. We need to focus on improving everyone's lives, not just those of our kids. We should be striving for a country and world in which everyone does well. That doesn't mean we share everything equally or throw capitalism out the window. There can be different levels of "doing well." To thrive as a species, however, we need people to be safe. We need everyone to have access to things that keep them healthy, and we all need to have the same opportunities in life.

If we create innovative solutions to the world's problems, they need to be accessible to as many people as possible. Imagine that we create technologies that improve fuel consumption and decrease emissions. In an innovative, sustainable world, vehicles with that technology would be priced affordably. Then, more people could participate in lowering our emissions, and the world would keep on keeping on, delaying the apocalypse, and letting all of us move on to solving the next big problem.

CAPABLE OF CREATING CHANGE

My company, Truman's, makes cleaning products that reduce plastic consumption in the supply chain, so we're trying to make those products affordable for everyone. I take this responsibility seriously, in part, because I'm one of the lucky ones who does have the ability to create change. If inspired to do so, everyone who lives in a comfortable bubble could make a genuine difference to this world. I mean, owning a house isn't a prerequisite for doing good in the world. Anyone can contribute and create change. But it's easier to make a big impact when you're in a profession that touches a lot of lives. Doctors, lawyers, and business-people fall into that group. So do teachers, social workers, and a whole host of other people who aren't paid anywhere near enough.

But if you're reading this book, I'm guessing you've had some career success—at least on the surface. You've figured out how to support yourself and your family. You—and I—are uniquely positioned to make significant leaps forward in our organizations to improve the world for everyone. We just have to break free and actually do it.

And then, we can benefit our kids in a more direct way, as well as this "better for everyone" idea. Let's go back to that fictional family. If the mom's a lawyer and she's working to make the world a more just place, that's far more inspiring to the kids than knowing their mom practices law because it'll put them through college. If the doctor dad is working on cancer research because he believes families should not be torn apart by this disease, that's an amazing message for the kids. They're hearing stories of serving the broader community. They're learning there's more to life than the Xbox and PS4 and ski vacations on spring break. They're discovering the importance of contributing to the community.

ANCESTRAL INSPIRATION

My grandmother was a big contributor to the community. In later life, she brought people of all faiths together to serve her community. She was Jewish, and, back in World War II, when her homeland became unsafe for Jews, she made the heartbreaking decision to leave her house, her possessions, friends, and extended family, to escape persecution. Jews across Europe were under attack, and the United States felt like her only shot at safety.

She wasn't just worried about herself. Of course, she wanted to survive and live free, but it was about more than that. She wanted her future generations to have a better life than was likely under the Nazi regime. At the time, she didn't know what we now see: that had she stayed, she would have no future generations. Rumors were rampant, but she didn't know what was happening inside the concentration camps. For her, leaving was a risk. She wasn't escaping certain death; she was choosing a hard and unknown path for the chance to have a family, and for that family to have more safety, freedom, and opportunities than their elders. It was a risky move for a radical result.

She and her family broke out of Belarus and fled to the US via Japan. They didn't have visas. They did it all illegally. Illegal moves were better than the fate the Nazis had prepared for them. They received a lot of help as they fled for safety. Many strangers took risks to get them across borders and onto transit, including, most famously, Chiune Sugihara. Sugihara was a Japanese diplomat who helped six thousand Jews flee Europe during WWII. He was later honored with many titles, monuments, awards, and books written about his efforts.

This experience gave my grandmother a deeply held belief that *people help people*. It doesn't matter if they're Christian like Sugihara, Jewish, atheist, or anything else. She took a holistic attitude. She saw that luck contributed to her arrival in the US. She knew timing had played a role. She believed that you must work hard in life, but help is always available—and from people of all faiths.

Once she settled in the US, she could've dwelled on the home she'd left, the struggles she endured, and the family members who'd been killed. But she didn't. I'm sure there were times when she struggled with those thoughts, but she focused her efforts on paying it forward. She appreciated that a diverse group helped her escape, and a new country embraced her, so she worked to bring diverse people together for good. She tried to have a positive impact on the community that surrounded her, volunteering her time with local charities and creating a group-sourced, interfaith cookbook to bring people together in a new way. She worked on that cookbook during her final years, when she was battling illnesses. I always thought that said a lot about her constant focus on bringing people together and preserving what makes us all so unique. That extended to caring for her family; even though my father didn't live close by when my brother and I grew up, my grandmother lived closer and connected with her grandkids.

VARIED VIEWPOINTS

It's easy to look at the course of my grandmother's life and think, *Of course she paid it forward. What else would she do?* But hers isn't the approach everyone takes. Each immigrant has their own experiences and their own perception of them. Hell, every person—whether they've fled across the world or never left their hometown—has their own take on their experiences. People aren't defined by their backgrounds; every individual chooses how to filter their experiences and distill them into action.

My grandfather, on the other side of my family, also fled

Europe around that time. He and my grandmother left Austria and made their way to the US. I don't know as much of their story. My grandfather didn't like to talk about the journey. I do know he filtered his experiences into a fervent desire to look after his own. His whole existence revolved around providing for his daughter—my mom—and his grandsons—me and my brother. In his imperfect English, he'd tell me, "These things are tough, but everything I do is for your mother and you boys."

I'm grateful that he looked after our family so well. I also feel sad when I remember him. He didn't have many friends. He didn't have parents and siblings he could interact with. He didn't look out into the world. He did a great job in helping my mom raise my brother and me, but his was a smaller life, and I'm not sure it was a fulfilling one.

Back when my grandfather had recently arrived in the US, his wife gave birth to my mom and then passed away. He found himself a new immigrant forced to raise a baby alone. In an odd twist of events, he became friends with three sisters who volunteered to help raise his little girl. Helen, Dottie, and Louise became family, stepping in to care for my mom while my grandfather worked.

Many years later, when my mom became a single parent, these wonderful women, then in their seventies, stepped in again. They helped raise my brother and me. I remember them wrapping me in a blanket and swinging me around in it. I slept at their house every night. They read me stories and put me to bed while Mom worked the night shift. Mom was also studying, trying to create a better life for us, so these three women were my primary caregivers, day and night.

And they were wonderful. They supported me in whatever I was interested in. When I announced I liked drawing, they said, "We'll give you five cents for every picture you make." The next thing they knew, their house was filled with drawings, and my pockets spilled over with nickels.

Helen, Dottie, and Louise were of African American and Native American heritage. They were born in Massachusetts in the early 1900s. They obviously didn't share my grandparents' experiences of Nazi persecution, but they faced tremendous racism in their lives.

LOOKING OUT, REGARDLESS

All of the grandparental figures in my life were challenged by the same theme: hardship based on a variable outside their control. My grandparents were Jewish. The ladies who raised me were women of color. Through them all, I saw wildly different interpretations of how the same theme can impact people. I saw them respond in completely different ways in their daily lives, and in the lessons they passed on to me. One taught me about looking after family. Another demonstrated the importance of community. And then, there was the lesson of dreaming big.

This tells me that neither hardships nor successes translate into defined attitudes. We can choose what we take from our experiences. I have chosen my paternal grandmother's community-minded approach. People help people. Not always and not everywhere, certainly, but \ when times are tough, there is help out there for those who seek it. Her story is evidence of this. She traveled across the world with very little money and was graced by other people's inclusiveness, acceptance, and embracing of diversity. And hers is not an isolated event; anytime the world finds itself in crisis, there are stories of good all around.

Whatever our circumstances, however we ended up in our comfortable bubbles, we need to look up and reach out. We cannot continue to live isolated lives, doing nothing but ensuring our kids will be okay. If that's all we focus on, they will end up well-loved, well-educated, and surrounded by a disintegrating world. Our kids can only thrive if the world around them survives. That means we—the people most able to impact our communities—must act to sustain everyone through war, political unrest, pandemics, pollution, or whatever else we face. We can't assume someone else will solve all these issues. It's *our* responsibility to kick the country out of stagnation and into an innovative, solutions-based future.

CHAPTER TWO

MEASURING UP TO MAMMOTHS

Elon Musk thinks big. If you don't know him, he's a crazy-successful innovator and entrepreneur who's best known for co-founding a company called Tesla. Tesla has arguably created the most innovative product to come out of the transportation industry in decades: a *desirable* electric car.

How did he do it? He thought big. I mean, the cars themselves aren't that big—although the Cybertruck model has a ton of storage. But his ideas were massive. He imagined making the electric vehicle a luxury item, not a cheap, hippy gimmick, as some people had previously perceived it. (For what it's worth, I like electric cars. My wife drove a Prius for nine years.) Tesla is still working on making itself profitable. Still, it's on track because people aspire to buy these high-performing, fashion-symbol, electric vehicles—which happen to be good for the environment.

The electric car has been around since the 1880s, but before Elon Musk and Tesla, no one could successfully mass produce. There were too many infrastructure challenges involved in creating a non-gasoline, non-diesel vehicle. Musk came up with innovative ways to solve those challenges on multiple fronts. He solved the infrastructure issues. Then, he solved the challenges around positioning the car in the market, so people actually wanted the cars. He developed the technology. He patented their results. He built the brand. And he solved for the million other challenges that surely came with doing something new and disruptive, all in a relatively short amount of time; Tesla was founded in 2003. By comparison, Ford was launched in 1903, Chevrolet in 1911, and Jeep in 1941.

While changing the landscape of the transportation industry, Elon Musk has also been running some other small projects, such as founding SpaceX, a private aerospace company whose goal is to prevent human extinction by enabling the colonization of Mars. Another small project? A neuro-technology company that's developing brain implants to help people communicate their thoughts directly to computers.

Another of his businesses, The Boring Company, apparently started when Musk was driven nuts by Los Angeles traffic and threatened to dig a massive tunnel under the city to lessen the traffic hell above ground. According to the urban myth, it was supposed to be a joke, but here we are, and The Boring Company is now digging a big old hole under LA. He was named one of the world's most powerful people by *Forbes*, his net worth is valued at around $27.9 billion, and, in 2018, he launched his car into space. (Google "Where is Starman?" to track the car's orbit.)

Clearly, Musk is an elephant who knows his strength. He refuses to be held back by traditional norms. He laughs in the face of common-sense facts, such as "cars drive on roads." No, he looks at a car and thinks, *Why not drive this baby through a labyrinth of underground tunnels? Why can't we fly this thing through space?* He doesn't let his experiences to date dictate his future.

Most people look at someone like Musk and say, "I could never do that. Even if I worked for an auto manufacturer/ NASA/a tunnel developer/a launching-cars-into-space-company, I couldn't have come up with that kind of innovation. I couldn't look into the future that way." And they'd be right. There's only one Elon Musk. I sure as hell can't compete with him, and neither can many others.

So, most people don't try. Most folks think if they can't innovate like the Elon Musks of the world, they can't innovate, period. They assume they're just not one of "those people." They're not someone who can do interesting things or drive the world forward or improve people's lives. They can't break free.

But breaking free does not require you to think as big as Musk. And you don't need a spare car lying around that you're happy to shoot into space. Many comparatively unknown people have broken free from the usual expectations and are driving innovation forward in fascinating ways.

Take the small Canadian company Plastic Bank, for example. They've created plastic recycling operations in places like Indonesia, Haiti, and the Philippines, where plastic pollution is a real problem. Recycling operations exist in these areas, but there's no incentive for locals to participate. Dumping plastic trash on roadsides and in waterways is easy, convenient, and commonly accepted behavior, so why should they do otherwise?

Here's where Plastic Bank innovated the industry: *They created an incentive.* They are a literal bank converting plastic into currency. Anyone can pick up plastic bags, bottles, and other items, take them to a Plastic Bank facility, and get paid for their efforts. The bank can afford to pay for plastic deposits because they, in turn, sell that plastic to manufacturers who want the items for the resin within. They recycle that resin and use it for their products, as it's cheaper than creating resin from scratch.

In poverty-stricken places, any opportunity for locals to earn money is highly valuable. But this process offers value on every angle. The streets and oceans are cleaned up, locals make money, manufacturers get a good deal, and everyone becomes more aware of the environmental issues with pollution. It's value for all.

The project was founded by David Katz and Shaun Frankson, two men with game-changing ideas and zero cars floating in orbit. They started the program in a very organic, small-scale way, and increased its operations as its success grew. Compare that to the way Musk is trying to find solutions to space travel challenges. I haven't studied their balance sheet, but I'm betting building and launching a space rocket costs a little more than building a recycling shack on the beach. One was a multimillion-dollar bet that would either work wonders or explode into a massive fireball. The other took a few two-by-four timbers and a volunteer willing to stand in the sun.

However, I would argue that both projects are incredibly innovative, and both will be impactful as they grow, scale, and improve our world. So sure, if you have billions of dollars to throw around, feel free to build a colony on Mars or some other crazy shit. But you don't need Elon Musk's money or status or genius to make a difference in the world. You can do it in an attainable, low-risk way. With the right idea and the willingness to try, you can start by standing on a beach.

A SMALL ELEPHANT IN A MAMMOTH COMPANY

Unfortunately, most people in corporate America don't get much time on the beach. They're chained to their desks in a gray office block somewhere. This is where I found myself in the fall of 2013. Eight years earlier, after graduating from business school, I'd been lucky enough to score a place in GE's leadership training program. After two years, I joined GE Appliances and worked my way up the ranks of the company pretty quickly. By the time summer wrapped in 2013, I was working directly for Beth Comstock in GE's business innovations group. Beth was the first female vice chair of the company, and I was privileged to learn from her. We worked on consumer venture projects and trademark licensing initiatives and got to reimagine what we could be from a marketing and business innovation perspective.

It was a cool role, but I came to it at a tough time in GE's history. The company was going through a massive transformation, trying to figure out the most effective organizational structure after taking on a bunch of acquisitions, and it kind of lost its way. It's a challenge that big businesses sometimes face.

And GE was mammoth; I was one of three hundred thousand employees. In that environment, it's hard to see the direct impact of your work. I knew our group did good work, but there was so much happening around us that it felt like our efforts were sucked into this big, bureaucratic machine where they just...disintegrated. We were trying to drive innovation, but we were like a single cog pushing hopelessly against a huge metal beast.

Of course, when you're not the top dog, it's easy to sit at your desk and think, *God, if I were running this place, I'd do all this differently.* I did my fair share of that. But then it went further. I got to the point where I really wanted the chance to run things the way I imagined. I can see you rolling your eyes at me, and sure, it might've been the classic case of the critic thinking they can do better. But I didn't just want to do things *my way* for the sake of waving my amazing achievements in GE's face. You'll just have to believe me on that. I was driven to try something new because I could see how an organization that was truly sustainable and innovative could have a more positive impact on its people and the world. And that's the kind of impact I was craving.

I also wanted to explore business philosophies that seemed risky to a company steeped in tradition. I wanted to break free of the constraints of that tradition and try something new. I wanted to play with the idea of speed. At GE, I'd helped the company invest in some small businesses. I loved watching these portfolio companies work. They were fast. Compared to GE, they moved at lightning speed. We had might and power and obscene amounts of money, but we couldn't keep up with these companies that were a fraction of our size. I realized that to make the kind of impact I craved I'd have to move fast in whatever I chose to do.

I was fascinated with the concept of driving innovation in disruptive technologies. GE had plenty of interesting avenues, but they couldn't move fast enough to innovate the industries it worked within. It was so weighed down with infrastructure and assets that we couldn't look beyond systems that utilized those assets. We slipped into always operating within the structure we'd created. That meant new ideas were limited and not that revolutionary.

In the end, I realized I could accomplish more outside of GE than within its walls. I was frustrated that I couldn't have more impact on the company, and I felt like I'd given all I could within the limits of a big business infrastructure. I was done with meetings and more meetings and unread emails and work that just drives more work. Life is short, and as the years ticked by, I found myself reflecting. When I eventually reach the end of my days, was this the work I'd be proud of? As I didn't feel like I was making any difference anymore, the answer was an easy no.

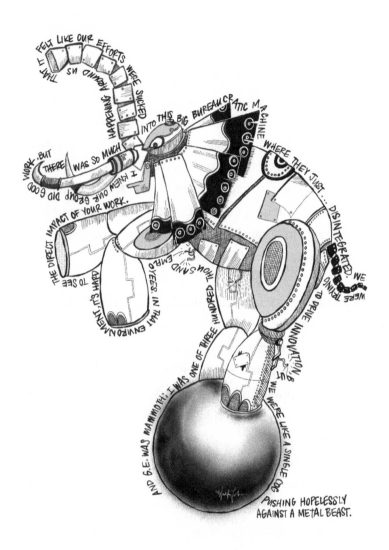

THAT IT FELT LIKE OUR EFFORTS WERE SUCKED INTO THIS BIG BUREAUCRATIC MACHINE WHERE THEY JUST... DISINTEGRATED. WE WERE TRYING TO DRIVE INNOVATION B UT WE WERE LIKE A SINGLE DOG PUSHING HOPELESSLY AGAINST A METAL BEAST.

WORK. BUT THERE WAS SO MUCH HAPPENING AROUND US

I KNEW OUR GROUP DID GOOD WORK. IT'S HARD TO SEE THE DIRECT IMPACT OF YOUR WORK. IN THAT ENVIRONMENT.

AND G.E. WAS MAMMOTH: I WAS ONE OF THREE HUNDRED THOUSAND EMPLOYEES.

LEARNING TO TAKE RISKS

Leaving felt like a risk. It was the latest in a series of increasing experiments I took at work. These weren't exactly Elon Musk-type risks, but I had managed to graduate somewhat from my big leap in reimagining microwave menu systems. That goofy step with the microwave product line had been my first launch into forward movement. From there, I'd gained confidence, even within the constraints of a big company. But I was lucky; the confidence that grew over my career was seeded in me from a young age.

The elderly women who raised me—Helen, Dottie, and Louise—used to tell me we could do anything we wanted in this world. With racism as it was in mid-twentieth-century Massachusetts, some would've said they *couldn't* do whatever they wanted, and it was foolish to teach that mentality to a child—even if that child was a sandy-haired white kid.

But they persisted. In ways that were appropriate to my age, they pointed out racism in our little town. They taught me to notice the small things, good and bad, and to pay attention to my surroundings. They showed me how to be mindful of the impact of my actions. They raised me to treat others with respect, understanding that our behavior can impact many people. They reminded me constantly that I could choose how I acted and impacted others. They planted a seed of confidence that I could grow up to do anything I wanted.

When I was at business school, Deb Elam, GE's former chief diversity officer, gave a compelling speech in which she talked about GE's desire to solve big, world problems. Afterward, I connected with her and was impressed by what she said about the company. That interaction inspired me to apply to GE's leadership program, which set my career path. Elam was right—GE was trying to impact the world for good. It was true then, and, I believe, it remained true even to the day I left. The mammoth company just lost its way for a while. But back as a fresh-faced MBA graduate, I was attracted to the company's desire to be deliberate in how it impacted others.

I signed up and, over the years, grew the confidence I'd inherited from those who raised me. I took a little risk with a microwave oven line, and it was *a little* risk. The project's budget didn't exactly match what Elon Musk spent on his space adventures. Individually, I was invested in the idea, but I didn't have any actual investors knocking down the door with their financial analysts in tow. Who knows— maybe I'd have been shot in the head if the initiative didn't go down well? That assumes the senior execs even noticed my work. More likely, no one was going to lose their job (or sleep) over my microwave menu gamble. It felt like a leap in my career to do something new and "out there," but it wasn't exactly a big-time risk.

But it was a small leap that helped me grow my risk profile. A risk profile isn't like a stock portfolio or a cholesterol measurement; there's no assigned number that tracks your risk profile over time. It's just a way of talking about how confident you are in taking risks. My risk profile is relatively high, meaning I tolerate risky behavior well. After all, I am the guy who risked it all on a microwave menu system, don't you know?

I laugh at myself now, but for me, at the time, that did feel risky. And then, my risk tolerance grew, and I tried other new things. I spoke up more in meetings. I pushed the boundaries of innovation within the constraints of the business. I tugged on the chain around my ankle—and hard. Eventually, I broke free and changed the future of a midsized company, then launched my own small business, Truman's, in one of the most entrenched industries in America.

ELON IS NOT THE ANSWER

When my business partner, Alex, and I started researching the ideas that would become Truman's, we realized that the cleaning industry has remained largely unchanged since the dawn of soap. But it's certainly not the only industry in modern America that's stuck in the dark ages.

Sure, we have more startups, technological advancements, apps, and interesting ideas in the world, but we also have more big businesses than ever before. As I learned the hard way at GE, these large companies are not agile or innovative. They create enormous groups of employees who feel like they could be doing more but are unable—or unwilling—to actually implement change. They see the Elon Musks of the world and think we, as a species, are doing okay. We're sending cars into space, for god's sake. Isn't that progress for humankind?

But a handful of high-profile, innovative people and companies blind us to the reality: We are not innovating at the rate the world requires. We're not creating sustainable solutions to the world's ever-growing problems. Air pollution, pandemics, food shortages, contaminated waterways, and even school shootings are all getting worse, and our businesses are not tackling these challenges. The States has long been a proud land of capitalism, but the companies that run our commerce-driven country are failing to tackle the challenges of our modern world.

Elon is not the answer. He's about the most impressive man I can think of, and yes, I'm jealous of his car collection. But the world doesn't need a million Elon Musks. It just needs people to improve the world around them. Perhaps that's more CEOs starting non-profit organizations. Or engineers creating new versions of their products using fewer materials. Or department heads developing eco-friendly policies.

Wherever you're at, break free from there. Shake off the chains of life as you know it, and imagine what would happen if you innovated in this world. We'll talk more about how to ignite your imagination later in this book, but know that innovation begins with breaking free from the norms. That doesn't require you to climb the mountain to Elon Musk heights. It means starting with a single step.

CHAPTER THREE

TUGGING THE CHAIN

I'm proud to say that my current company, Truman's, is truly innovative. It's changing an entrenched industry by drastically reducing plastic consumption and toxicity in homes. It wasn't easy to design an entirely new concept for cleaning products. It required a giant leap from the "normal way" of doing things. I am so glad, though, that we took that leap, and we were willing to try something new. Our cleaning cartridge system is unique in the industry.

When I was considering leaving GE, I wasn't ready to do something as unconventional as Truman's. That required breaking free from corporate America and becoming an entrepreneur, as well as doing new things in an old industry. At the time, I couldn't imagine that. So, I took a midsized leap into a smaller, more agile corporate company, in which I could have a real impact on its sustainability. The company I chose was Big Ass Fans.

I actually discovered them through my work with GE. We were doing a lot to learn from startup companies. Beth, my boss, challenged us to take a break from our everyday work to go see companies that did things differently. Someone on our team had met with Big Ass Fans and came back raving about how interesting and innovative they were. I wanted to learn what they were doing to give my colleague such a crush, and I was curious about the kind of professional who would call his company Big Ass Fans. So, I went to meet the man.

This wasn't long after my ten-year anniversary with GE. I was genuinely shocked when I realized I'd spent a decade of my life there. When I started, I thought the job would be a springboard into something really interesting and impactful. But now I was the general manager of consumer ventures, which was fine. It paid a good salary, but I wasn't exactly saving the world.

The company gave me a plaque to commemorate my ten-year anniversary. Maybe some people like those kinds of goofy gifts, but for me, it was a *holy shit* moment. I realized a decade had flown by. The job had allowed me to do my duty and support my family, but I felt a greater calling to do more interesting, impactful work. GE was an interesting company, but it felt like my primary role was to keep doing the same old thing. I was just a battered old cog buried in the depths of an immense machine.

I left the plaque in a hotel room on one of my many trips to New York, far from my family in Kentucky. I had no interest in keeping a token that reminded me of all the times I'd felt the pull to leave but been dragged back in with another minor distraction. Big companies do a really good job of keeping you just busy enough, distracted enough, tired enough that you don't look for more fulfilling work elsewhere. Their business life cycles keep pulling you back in, engaging you in challenging work that doesn't really affect much change. They cycle you through various opportunities that make you feel good for a short while, so you can push down the urge to do more meaningful work and snuff it out.

As I'd cycled through my ten-year stint, I'd had some great accomplishments in the context of GE. From a career perspective, I'd done very well. But when I thought about the greater world, I was left questioning my contribution. What had I accomplished outside of the company? Had it been worthwhile to devote so much of my life to one entity? And if I did have the courage to leave, what the hell would I even do?

MEETING THE LEGEND

All these thoughts were running through my head as I drove to the Big Ass Fans headquarters in the heart of Lexington, Kentucky's, horse farm country. I was there to meet the company's founder, Carey Smith, and take inspiration and ideas back to GE. Lexington made me think of sprawling farmland, horses galloping into the sunset, beautiful barns and hand-built ranches, picket fences, and all that other old-world bullshit. So, when I pulled up in the parking lot, ready for my meeting with Carey, I was caught off guard.

Their building was modern. Edgy. Contemporary. It was surrounded by the flags of all the countries where they did business. I went inside, introduced myself, and was led upstairs to a conference room. As I walked along behind the receptionist, I was struck by the wide, open space where everyone worked together. There were no closed offices. Only the meeting rooms were behind closed doors. The whole place just felt...cool. Everything about it was the opposite of GE, even though I thought it was the type of place GE wanted to be. I was led into a room called Boardwalk. (All the meeting spaces were named for Monopoly properties.) And then Carey Smith came in.

His gray hair was neatly parted, his beard was close trimmed, and his glasses glinted in the sunlight flooding into the room. He wore a button-down shirt with the Big Ass Fans logo in the corner. He shook my hand and smiled—a big, genuine smile that reflected in his eyes. Immediately, I got the sense that he was a friendly guy.

Then, he told me that the GE team was a bunch of buffoons who didn't know what they were doing.

"You know I work for GE?" I said.

"Yeah," he said with a shrug, before telling me his company was a thousand times better than mine and that his people were a thousand times smarter.

But weirdly, I wasn't offended. I was *impressed*. Here was a guy who loved his company. He was boisterous, sure. I knew people called him "insanely arrogant." Me, though? I thought he was confident. Incredibly confident. And it was fun to watch.

It worked, I think, because Carey wasn't shy. He talked—a lot—and I realized he was a very interesting individual. Our conversation showed me he was clearly well-read, bright, and spirited. And he'd proven his business acumen in the twenty years since starting his company. I was attracted to his vision for Big Ass Fans. He talked about setting the place up so it could be around for a couple of hundred years. He wanted to create something that would last.

I left Boardwalk that day thinking, *Wow, this is something special.* And I went back to my desk at GE and did nothing about it beyond sharing his ideas with my group. We considered steps to introduce some of their agility into our business. The ideas were good, but in a slow-moving company like ours, they didn't lead to much.

Over the coming months, I met with Carey Smith many more times. Eventually, our conversations turned to his biggest challenge: how to transition from a founder-led company to a more sustainable operating environment that didn't rely on his presence. He wanted to ensure his business would be around long after he moved on. Because he had been so involved in its operations for so long, I could tell it would be incredibly challenging to extricate him while ensuring the company remained strong. If Carey could create a company that could sustain itself throughout any change or challenge, that would define his legacy.

I was super excited at the prospect of being involved in such a unique opportunity. This was about real business sustainability. I don't mean "sustainable" in the environmentally friendly sense but as a business term. It was about adjusting operations so they could sustain changes in ownership and management and the world. Ensuring a company is sustainable in those terms has a positive impact on employees, the local community, and the brand. Plus, I thought it'd be fun as hell to work with Carey. His company had a quirky, fast-moving culture that was edgy and irreverent. It felt good to be there. I stopped feeling stagnant.

STEPPING OUT OF STAGNATION

Stagnation is the killer of dreams. Maybe that's how you feel in your work: idle and listless, like you're incapable of moving anywhere more meaningful. It's a common trap. I have a friend who's stuck in a rut. Every so often, he gets dissatisfied with work and looks around for something else. He looks at similar jobs that pay slightly more, but he's unwilling to even consider a larger leap into work that will have more of an impact on the world.

When I left the comfort of GE, I wasn't ready to make a truly massive leap. At the time, it was too much to imagine taking the steps required to start my own business or do innovative things in a challenging industry. Going to Big Ass Fans was a step out of stagnation and into movement. It was the essential step that eventually made Truman's feel possible.

It wasn't a quick decision, either. Significant steps are rarely easy. Breaking free of a known existence—even one that's kind of a downer—feels risky, and it often takes time to step into that. I'd be leaving a great pension plan, some significant stock options, a network of contacts I'd built over a decade, and a reputation within an industry I knew inside-out. At one point in mine and Carey's conversations, I actually wrote him a note asking for some time to think his offer through. By then, he'd asked me to come on board as chief operations officer to shepherd the transition into a more sustainable business model. I was almost ready, but it felt like a big step out of comfort and into the unknown.

After that, he suggested we have dinner with our wives. It turned into a long meal. We sat talking over dessert for about three hours. And then, I was sold. Yet again, I'd been blown away by his charisma and care for the company. I knew this wasn't the big leap that would help me save lives or solve the pollution problem or anything important on a global scale. But I admired what he'd built and wanted to help it last. This was a path to feeling better about my contribution to the world.

It wasn't exactly a shocker for Beth and the rest of my GE group when I left. They knew I wasn't excited about my future options there, and I'd been open with the leadership about my drive to do something more world changing. I think they were kind of delighted when I announced I was leaping into an obscure, small business with a funny name. So, I left the multibillion-dollar company with three hundred thousand employees and joined Big Ass Fans, which brought in a couple of hundred million dollars a year and had a staff of 1,300. It wasn't quite a ma-and-pa shop, but it felt that way to me.

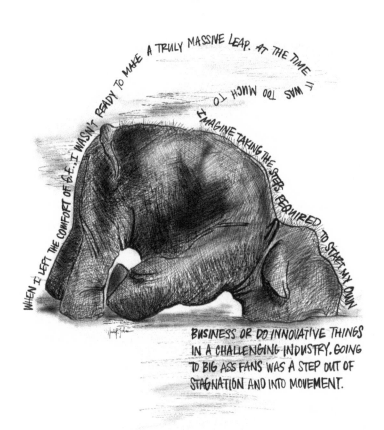

WHEN I LEFT THE COMFORT OF B.E., I WASN'T READY TO MAKE A TRULY MASSIVE LEAP. AT THE TIME IT WAS TOO MUCH TO IMAGINE TAKING THE STEPS REQUIRED TO START MY OWN BUSINESS OR DO INNOVATIVE THINGS IN A CHALLENGING INDUSTRY. GOING TO BIG ASS FANS WAS A STEP OUT OF STAGNATION AND INTO MOVEMENT.

AIM BIG BUT START SMALL

If you don't feel you can take a big step forward into something different—as I felt about something like Truman's—a smaller step is essential. Breaking free and finding more fulfilling work starts with pulling on the chain, just a little, to test your strength.

That's all you can reasonably expect to start with if you've spent your whole life being risk-averse, getting up at the same time every day, wearing the same color pants, putting on the right sock first, then the left, getting into your safety-rated sedan, and clocking in at a nice, secure company. If that's you, then god forbid you wear your gray pants with blue socks instead of the standard black socks. My goodness, the world would end—because it's not laundry day until Thursday, and you can't wash your socks on the wrong day of the week.

If that's you, then start with something that *feels* crazy: wear red socks with your gray pants. I dare you. And hell, if that's your starting point, then great. Recognize that and build up from there. Start with the step that feels radical to you, even if it's small by other people's standards. Because screw other people. This is your life. Your achievements. Your sense of contribution to the world.

In the grand scheme of world-changing events, my shiny new "broccoli" buttons on a microwave menu system was a baby step into a better world contribution. But to me, at the time, it was the most interesting thing I'd done in years. And it led down a path of successively bigger, more impactful decisions until I reached the point I'm at now, where people ask why I did something as crazy as starting my own company. "Why didn't you just go consult?" they ask. "How come you didn't go back to big business?"

The answer is that what looks risky to them feels like small beans to me now.

And that's the only path forward for anyone. Understand where the hell you are in terms of risk-taking and start making decisions that push you forward from there. There's no inventory process to assess your current risk profile. There isn't a neat little five-point plan to become more risk-tolerant. You just start moving. I can't promise you those moves will pay off, but you're not going to be thrown in jail for quitting one six-figure salary for another.

WHEN RISKS DO—OR DON'T—PAY OFF

Luckily for me, the move to Big Ass Fans did pay off. When I arrived, I discovered the company ultimately wanted to be like GE down the road. I spent a lot of time really understanding how the organization worked and where there were opportunities to improve, simplify, and set it up to make sense for the future. With Carey, I looked at the business intimately and holistically. We talked about strategic options. Within six months, we settled on a direction and started executing the plan to sell the company to a firm that would be able to fund and grow it into the future.

In less than two years, we closed a transaction to sell Big Ass Fans to a private equity firm for $500 million—a phenomenal price for a business of its nature. A lot of people were surprised by how much we secured, and they weren't shy in saying so. It was an extraordinary event for us, for the city of Lexington, and even for the state of Kentucky. Carey took an exit as a founder. He made a shit-load of money and paid out a ton to the employees, which had always been an essential part of the plan. I made a decent chunk of cash, too, making the risk of leaving GE literally pay off. With the sale, we felt confident the company would now live beyond its founder. It started its shift from "the Carey Smith show" to an independently sustainable, high-performing program.

Risks don't always pan out with a big paycheck and a pat on the back from the city of Lexington. Sometimes they don't work out. That's why they're called risks. Breaking free from the norm to do something different will always feel hazardous, to a degree. It inevitably involves swings and misses. Some moves don't play out well, but a few do. When you swing and score big, you feel like you did something important. You moved in the direction you believe in, and you contributed in a noteworthy way to the world. And that gives you a kind of rush.

Even if things don't pan out, you learn from those experiences. You feel how empowering it is to impact the world around you. You're inspired. You gain confidence. You just feel good about yourself. And god knows, we could all do with more of that. When your risk does work out, you get the rush of recognizing you made a positive impact, and you want to do it again. You train yourself to be more risk-tolerant because the rewards are so fulfilling.

So, start with gray pants and red socks. Break free from small expectations, know someone might laugh at your mismatched fashion choices, and keep doing it anyway. Create a reinforcing cycle of change that will move you from stagnation to satisfying payoffs. Before you know it, you'll be completely changing up your wardrobe. And then, you'll get to *choose* the impact you make on the world. That's what we'll talk about next.

CHAPTER FOUR

IDENTIFY YOUR IMPACT

Jeff Bezos is another modern-day mammoth. When he founded Amazon from his garage in 1994, he intended to solve the problems of accessibility of books. How could one individual have access to millions and millions of books? That was the question that drove him. Pre-internet, it simply hadn't been possible. You couldn't put a brick-and-mortar bookstore housing that many titles in every market. It just wouldn't make sense. And with the constraints of the retail supply chain, you couldn't make abstract books readily available.

Bezos understood how emerging technology could be applied in a unique way to solve these very complex issues. He saw that people wanted access to all kinds of books. He knew scale would be required to serve that demand, and, when he identified the growth of this new thing called "the internet," he imagined a way to bypass the physical barriers of the industry. I don't know Bezos personally, and I wasn't exactly sitting in his garage, watching him work through these ideas. But I imagine him there, all that time ago, thinking, *Wow. More and more people are going online. I think the internet might become mainstream.* Clearly, he saw how this new platform could act as a vehicle to change the way products and services are bought and sold.

He then built out those ideas brilliantly. He took a tired old product category—books—and used the online experience to enhance it. Thanks to the physical constraints on bookstore sizes and the sheer number of books in existence, I don't think he could've chosen a better product category. It wasn't just difficult to obtain obscure books, but there was no elegant way to learn about them, read reviews, or connect with others who'd read them already. Life was impossible before the internet.

By leaping on fast-growing technology, Bezos solved these issues ingeniously. Through Amazon, it was incredibly easy to access those random books. Published works that had previously struggled to find shelf space now had a new lease on life. Booklovers—and soon everyone—were enamored, and physical bookstores just couldn't compete. As I write, we all know Amazon as the world's largest online marketplace, which has expanded to offer cloud technology services, digital streaming, and artificial intelligence, among many other things.

Bezos and Amazon have had their challenges, and they're certainly not infallible. I am so inspired, though, by the innovation Bezos brought to a previously stagnant industry. When this trendy internet thing was starting to shape the world, he identified an opportunity and leaped into action, using it to exponentially improve access to books.

THINK MACRO, NOT MICRO

Bezos gets a lot of bad press, and his companies—he has several in addition to Amazon—are often attacked in the media. Whatever the truth behind the criticisms, it's undeniable that Bezos has made a significant, positive contribution to this world. Amazon is the world's biggest online retailer, changing the landscape of publishing, retail, and numerous other industries.

He has made a macro difference. Compare this to countless corporations that try to inspire potential customers by sharing their "sustainability plans." They say shit like, "We're going to reduce energy consumption by 5 percent over the next five years." And that's pretty much all there is to their plan. Maybe they throw around a few other cute goals, but these things are just goofy. I mean, 5 percent over five years? Who's going to notice that? That isn't a real, authentic sustainability plan; it's a lame publicity stunt.

I don't expect everyone to be like Jeff Bezos, and the world doesn't need that, either. But come on. Most corporate styles of micro change aren't going to impact anyone. And I'll bet my red socks that no one in those companies is going home jumping for joy, babbling to their partner because they're so excited about the new sustainability initiatives and the difference they'll make with their 5 percent in five years.

To feel like your work is making a positive impact, you've actually got to make a noticeable, markedly positive impact. It's not enough to just nudge the scale. Yes, if you're not used to taking steps outside the normal way of doing things, you have to start small and get your confidence up. But then you need to look for bigger leaps. Aim to be Bezos, not the 5 percent person. And if you fall short, you'll still be beating out most corporations.

I would say this to anyone in my organization, anyone who considers me a mentor, and I'll say it to you: Really think about the contribution you want to make in this world. Identify the impact you want to make, then decide on the best outlet for that change. Choose your path to get there.

There are three main paths to take impactful business leaps: reimagining products and services, redesigning operations and supply chains, and aligning organizations into multidimensional sustainability. These three elements can elicit change in isolation, or they can be combined for greater effect. Let me explain through the prism of my favorite company: my own.

REIMAGINING PRODUCTS AND SERVICES

The idea for Truman's came when my business partner, Alex, and I were looking for our next venture. We'd worked together at Big Ass Fans and had recently closed the transaction to sell the company and transitioned it to the new owners. I'd done my job in restructuring the company and now felt more comfortable taking an even bigger leap. I was ready to invest in something more impactful.

So, Alex and I chose to build the coolest, sexiest product we could think of: kitchen cleaners. (We also have floor, shower, and glass cleaners, as well as laundry and dish-washer bars, but I don't want to over-excite you.) I knew nothing about the chemical compounds of cleaning products or the history of the industry. Still, I knew the cabinet under my kitchen sink was rammed with big-ass bottles of "sunshine meadows"-scented sprays and wipes and other shit that irritated my hands and made me worry that the kids would one day drink from them. (For the record, we've managed nine years without a single kid-poisoning in our house. My wife and I are very proud of ourselves.)

I also knew that when I walked down the cleaning aisle of my local grocery store, there were fifty-seven different types of cleaners to choose from. Yes, I counted. I found forty-three scents, including lemon verbena, mango mandarin burst, and fresh linen, and fifteen types of unique surface cleaners. When I was too overwhelmed to remember if my kitchen counters were granite or quartz—because god forbid, I got the wrong cleaner for the wrong surface—I tried ordering cleaning products online. I still had to choose from the obscene number of options available, but at least I could do it in my sweatpants from the comfort of my couch. And I was able to check on the countertops from there. They were quartz, in case you were wondering.

I felt pretty bad when the delivery box arrived. I realized I'd just had someone truck this box from a warehouse across countless miles to a distribution hub, into another vehicle, across more miles to a local shipper, who then schlepped it over to me. That wouldn't have bothered me too much except that I realized this delivery was about 98 percent water. All that effort, all those vehicle emissions, a huge carbon footprint, just to send me a bottle of water with a few chemicals. I have water in my kitchen faucet. All I really needed was the cleaning stuff, and I could've mixed it myself.

This realization came as Alex and I were actively looking for an industry in need of innovation. We wanted to make our mark on the planet, and, as husbands and dads involved in the day-to-day running of our families, these issues literally hit home for us. When we paired those challenges with the knowledge that all these sprays come in single-use bottles, which just add to the world's plastic pollution problem, we saw a product that needed reimagining.

Kitchen cleaners had, to our minds, three problems: a difficult buying process with too many choices, toxicity concerns that made us uncomfortable using the products around our kids and letting the run-off stream into the waterways, and the huge carbon footprint involved in the supply chain of single-use bottles filled mostly with water. It became our mission to reimagine how this category could look if these problems were solved. You can do this, too. No, I don't mean you should trawl the aisles of grocery stores counting cleaning products like a crazy guy. You can identify a product or service that needs fixing. Find a problem to solve and make that your mission.

REDESIGNING OPERATIONS AND SUPPLY CHAINS

Sometimes a product or service is solid, but it's affected by problematic operations systems and supply chains. Have you ever received a package that's stuffed with bubble wrap to protect the contents? In our house, one of the kids grabs the sheet of bubble wrap and starts popping those air-filled bubbles. In the past, those sheets were manufactured in a facility where they filled the bubbles with air, then shipped them to packing facilities. Let's think about the insanity of this. They were shipping air. Literally *shipping air*. And, thanks to the increased size of the air-filled product, they were paying a premium for the pleasure.

Finally, someone with some common sense realized this was the dumbest thing on earth, and developed technology that allowed packers to fill their own bubble wrap with air. The technology was accessible, so even micro packers like small FedEx stores could take advantage of it. This led to a radical redesign of an operations and supply chain.

Once upon a time, rolls of air-filled bubble wrap were loaded into hundreds of trucks, which cost time, fuel, drivers' wages, and emissions to transport across the country. Now, the same number of sheets can be transported with a fraction of the vehicles, workforce, and pollution, and quickly filled on-site by packers as they need it.

Alex and I thought this radical restructuring of an operations and supply chain was inspiring. It was pretty clear how we could apply this to our cleaning products idea. So now, we ship cleaning liquids in concentrated form, and the customer uses water from their own kitchen faucet to dilute the product. We use this cool cartridge design, which makes it easy (and—I'm not lying—kind of fun) to dilute the product into reusable bottles.

By only shipping concentrate, not water, we shrunk the supply chain by more than 70 percent. Where it would take thirty trucks to ship our competitors' product, you can transport the same end-use quantity of our product in one single truck. That saves an insane amount of money and emissions, making both our business and the world more sustainable. That's a win for everyone. (Unless you hate money and the earth. Then it's a loss for you.)

ALIGNING ORGANIZATIONS INTO MULTIDIMENSIONAL SUSTAINABILITY

Our company, Truman's, is somewhat radical. We could've created pre-diluted cleaning products packaged in recycled plastics collected from polluted oceans, but that would be a micro improvement. We'd still be shipping a product that's 98 percent water. Instead, by selling concentrate, we're reducing water consumption, reducing plastic use, shrinking supply chains, and massively shifting the way cleaning products are supplied, sold, and used. We're taking a radical, multidimensional approach to sustainability.

Our ideas aren't entirely new; think of your local Starbucks, for example. Alex and I spent a lot of time at Starbucks when brainstorming our ideas for Truman's. They don't use pre-mixed cleaning products. Each store receives massive bottles of concentrate, which staff dilute into reusable bottles. The same is true throughout the hospitality industry. So, we didn't reinvent the wheel but adapted this idea for another sector—the home cleaning industry. That was a radical move. It solves challenges throughout the end-to-end process; that's a multidimensional approach. And it does so in a way that can continue long-term; there's the sustainability. Truman's has a long way to go, but if even a tiny percentage of homeowners switch to our cleaning products, our impact will revolutionize the industry.

When you focus on aligning with multidimensional sustainability, you find radical answers to challenges in our world. For example, Alex and I recently spoke to someone who asked if our company would consider offering a disinfectant product. With the rise of the novel coronavirus, there was a sudden and enormous need for homeowners to have access to reliable disinfectants. Now, remember, we're a non-toxic cleaning company, and many disinfectants require toxic ingredients. On the face of it, our answer should've been no. But we prioritize *multidimensional* sustainability, so we looked at all the variables involved.

We started our non-toxic cleaning company to contribute to a better world. When people worry about disinfecting their homes, of course they turn to powerful cleaning products. If we could create a disinfectant that had a more efficient supply chain, that used less plastic than other options, and that people were more comfortable using in their home, we would contribute to a better world. We won't necessarily meet the classic definition of "being green," but we'd continue to make a positive contribution to a fast-changing world. So, we told this person that we *would* consider creating a disinfectant if we could do it in a way that was sustainable across its variable elements.

When you consider how you'll make your organization more sustainable, take a multidimensional approach. Look at the materials your product requires, the travel your executives take, the labeling your product uses, and every other aspect that contributes to your organization and its goal. Align those elements, and you'll find new possibilities to make giant leaps in your industry.

CHOOSE YOUR OWN PATH

The key is to identify the impact you want to make and the best outlet for that change. Whether you reimagine products and services, redesign operations and supply chains, or align organizations into multidimensional sustainability, you can create a true competitive advantage that will likely increase your business's bottom line. More importantly for your sense of fulfillment, all approaches will benefit society. They are levers you can pull to change industries and, in turn, change the world.

Truman's is currently a small business but, having introduced multidimensional sustainability to Big Ass Fans, I've seen how satisfying it is to get a whole organization thinking and operating in a new way. Within small businesses or large, leaders can be a conduit for change that inspires others. Radical changes are radically fulfilling.

If that's something you want to pursue—and I argue it should be, for yourself and the world around you—you need to change the way you think. After identifying the available areas for impact, you need to imagine the possible changes you can make. And that's where whiteboarding comes in.

CHAPTER FIVE

IMAGINE CHANGE

I live in New Orleans, and our cab drivers are friendly. They get you where you need to go and keep their vehicles surprisingly clean. But for a long time, they faced challenges with operations and supply. If my wife and I went out for dinner on a Saturday night, it would take forever to find a cab to take us home. Solving this supply problem made Uber famous.

Uber, as you may know, is a peer-to-peer ride-sharing company. Anyone who owns a vehicle can apply to be an Uber driver. The idea is that in your downtime, you can log onto the app, offer your driving services, and be paired with a nearby person who needs a ride somewhere. Drivers can monetize an asset they already own—their car—and people trying to get from A to B have another option besides the traditional, often unavailable cab.

In essence, this is an asset-sharing business model. Uber, as a company, does not need to purchase fleets of vehicles and pay direct employees. They act as an agency connecting a person with an asset to a person requiring that asset. This has made them uber-successful. The company operates in almost eight hundred metropolitan areas worldwide, with more than twenty-two thousand drivers and 110 million users. It's also a disruptive business model. In many places, its popularity has decimated the traditional cab industry.

The disruption has happened, in large part, because the structure of Uber's business model is so wildly different from anything seen in this industry before. It's revolutionary. I wasn't there for the birth of the Uber idea, but the company's founders clearly approached the industry with a completely blank slate for imagining what was possible. I recommend this blank slate approach to you—I call it *whiteboarding.*

WHITEBOARDING

After you've identified the impact you want to make on the world, you need to imagine how you can create that change. You need to envision how you'll make products, services, and operations more sustainable, efficient, minimal, or whatever you're trying to do. To imagine anything remotely interesting, you first have to erase what you already know.

Get a whiteboard with nothing on it, and build the product,

service, or operation up from scratch. I mean this literally. Find yourself a real whiteboard and some dry erase pens. Bonus points if they're in fun colors. Then, don't put anything about the existing process on the whiteboard. Nothing.

Think about what you're trying to create as a piece of art. With art, you start with something that *isn't* what it becomes. You begin a painting with a blank canvas, a drawing with a blank page. Theoretically, you could take an old painting and build on it to create a new piece of art, and I bet I'll get hundreds of emails now from people showing me examples. But almost all artists begin with a blank canvas.

Solving problems is done best when you create without constraints. I'm not suggesting you ignore the obstacles completely. Every situation has very real limitations, processes, and challenges. But when you start with the foundations of an innovative idea, you can build the constraints into the image, and innovate on top of that. If you do it the other way, laying out all the current constraints first, you'll never see past them to create something new.

So, you start with a blank whiteboard, then write the impact you've identified for change. Let's take my shining moment in the microwave industry as an example. Let's say you read this incredibly sad article about obesity rates skyrocketing. Everyone's getting fat. Soon, no one will fit in their cars.

Only three people will fit on a bus at one time. You think, *Holy shit. This is bad. I have to help.*

You grab your dry erase pen and write on the whiteboard, *I want to be a part of fixing obesity rates.* Then you stand back and consider the best way to do that. You twiddle your thumbs, grab a coffee, and another, and finally come up with a list that you scrawl on the board. It includes everything you can think of that could help in the fight against obesity, as informed by the report you just read. *Access to healthy foods. Education. Active living. Microwaves. Diet programs. Food labeling. Health policies.*

One of those variables is microwaves. Well, you happen to be the leader of a microwave oven product line. This is an area where you can actually make an impact, so it's natural to focus here. Of course, you're not totally restricted to this. You could say, "You know what? Microwaves just aren't an exciting way to address obesity. I'm going to quit this stupid job and go work for Weight Watchers." And you could.

But what if you knew you weren't ready for that leap, or if you were excited to tackle obesity within the microwave world? Only at this point do you begin to look at your current constraints. In my example, the constraint is microwaves. You think, *How can I contribute to this effort in a way that makes sense for the environment and job that I have today?*

This takes you from the big picture goal—fixing obesity rates—to the reality of the constraints in front of you.

Then, you keep working the whiteboard. You step back and think about all the ways you could solve the issue with what's on the board. You twiddle your thumbs some more, drink another fifteen cups of coffee, and write all your ideas on the board with your trusty hot-pink dry erase pen. You keep cycling through this process until you have a plan that feels really exciting—and a little bit risky.

Now, what if you weren't a goofy microwave man? Let's imagine you're the CEO of Weight Watchers. You've got $50 million over the next three years to invest in a moon-shot project. What do you do? You start with the same whiteboarding process. In nice, big letters, you write, *I want to solve the obesity rate problem.* You list the variables that impact the issue. You add in any constraints—and there are always constraints to consider, even when throwing around the big bucks. Whiteboarding gets you clear on the issue, helps you bring it into the context of the world you partic-ipate in, and gives you the freedom to come up with ideas. It's simple but effective, and it avoids the common pitfalls of brainstorming meetings.

THE BRAINSTORMING TRAP

In a typical company, the leaders will identify an issue

that needs to be solved. They'll schedule a brainstorming meeting, and you'll walk into a conference room filled with people sitting in front of their laptops, barely paying attention. Except, that is, when it comes time to give feedback.

Someone has just finished presenting a boring-as-hell, incremental adjustment plan. It's based on the company's legacy systems, whether that's technical or manufacturing or whatever, and uses existing assets to try and address the problem. Now, everyone looks up from their laptops to offer "constructive" feedback on why the plan won't work.

"Well, that won't align with the manufacturing process we have in this factory."

"We're already using another material, and we can't change that."

"We'd have to talk to this other team because it impacts them in this way."

Everyone loses sight of the fact that, ultimately, both profit and non-profit entities are built to *solve something*. Companies aren't created to be slaves to their own systems.

Often, those systems are old. A lot of categories of services and physical products were created a long time ago. The car, as we know it, has been around for more than a hundred

years. Vacuums were first invented in 1901. They've iter-
ated over time, but the technology is largely based on really
old developments. In case you hadn't noticed, the world
has changed over the last century or so. If you don't force
yourself to erase everything you know about an old system,
you can't dream about how it would work with inputs that
exist today.

Let's go back to Uber. Fifty years ago, if you wanted to get
someone from point A to point B, you needed a taxi. But
how did the general public call for one? There were no cell
phones and no data plans. Drivers didn't even have those
huge car-phones back then. Cab companies solved this
communication challenge with radios and infrastructure
to support them. The public could call a main line to reach
a dispatcher. The dispatcher could relay the request, via
radio, to the taxi driver. That meant cab companies required
a fleet of vehicles with radios installed and drivers attached.
It was a solution that worked.

Fast-forward to today. If you're a cab company trying to
continue providing this service in an efficient way, what do
you do? How do you improve your setup to serve growing
cities with increasing congestion? Well, if you own a fleet of
vehicles with radios installed, you fixate on trying to make
use of your assets. And you *don't* create Uber.

You don't consider the modern realities of every person

having communication devices at their fingertips. You don't think, *If someone is standing at a street corner and wants to call a cab, they probably have their cell phone in their hands, and an unlimited data plan.* You don't consider the supply chain in a new way, and think, *There are underused vehicles already in the marketplace and drivers looking to make extra money, and maybe they're closer than this yellow car.*

Uber drivers *are* closer. Almost always. Uber is more efficient than traditional taxis from a customer perspective. They also utilize multipurpose vehicles. Drivers use their car for personal time as well as Uber work. That keeps costs low. There's significant investment required to keep the app and back-end systems running, but these are scalable projects that can easily be applied worldwide. Uber doesn't have to pay thirty dispatchers to answer phones in each city and hire more as they become busier.

Bullshit brainstorming meetings aren't enough when the world is constantly changing, when you're dealing with new inputs all the time, when you need truly innovative ideas to actually make an impact. You need to take it further. Start with a clean canvas. Then define the problem you're solving and establish the most efficient way of doing it. And believe that anything is possible.

ANYTHING IS POSSIBLE

When we look at the way the world has evolved, every period has experienced something shocking. Think of the formation of the United States—that was a bold and risky move. How about the ultrasound? Some of our ancestors thought it was the devil's work to see images of a baby before it was born. The Wright brothers terrified people with the idea of flight.

How about more modern shocks? It blows my mind that I can use an app on my phone to call a car to take me to the airport, then fly to Australia and use the same app to get another car to take me to my hotel. It also boggles my brain that someone can sell a banana with a piece of duct tape on it for $150,000, but it happened. Some artist is rolling around in cash after selling this masterpiece that's supposed to represent...well, I don't know what. Silenced bananas, or something.

If you play the game of what's *not* possible, you'll lose every time. Maybe you'd say, "I'd like to go to the sun someday." And the devil on your shoulder says, "That's not possible, dummy." Well, I don't want to sound completely insane, but how do you know Elon Musk won't design a material that could protect his car from the heat of the sun? People thought we'd never land on the moon. Others thought no one would ever call the moon landing a conspiracy. But over the years, we've seen some pretty crazy things in every category and time frame you can name.

I believe in my bones that we need to look at everything in life as limitless. There are so many variables for any issue, and it's impossible to predict how they'll react with each other and what outcomes those reactions will bring. We should never assume we've got things all figured out. If we do, we'll stop pushing. Then we'll never get a car on the sun, or vacuums that don't clog up, or vaccines for every virus on earth.

I truly believe you can do anything you want to do. We'll get into how that works in upcoming chapters, but if you really want to find a way to achieve an impact, whiteboarding lets you see how that is possible. It lets you dream about doing things unencumbered by the bullshit that's been around for years and years. It frees you to move fast and in new directions. At Truman's, every day we act like there's a whiteboard in front of us. If we want to achieve something, we map out the best way to do so and don't let anything stop us. And I can tell you, I'm coming up with new ideas faster than ever before. With this approach, nothing holds us back. Anything is possible for us, and the same is true for you.

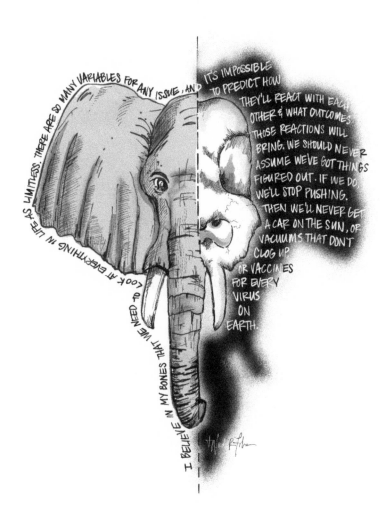

I BELIEVE IN MY BONES THAT WE NEED TO LOOK AT EVERYTHING IN LIFE AS LIMITLESS. THERE ARE SO MANY VARIABLES FOR ANY ISSUE, AND ITS IMPOSSIBLE TO PREDICT HOW THEY'LL REACT WITH EACH OTHER & WHAT OUTCOMES THOSE REACTIONS WILL BRING. WE SHOULD NEVER ASSUME WE'VE GOT THINGS FIGURED OUT. IF WE DO, WE'LL STOP PUSHING. THEN WE'LL NEVER GET A CAR ON THE SUN, OR VACUUMS THAT DON'T CLOG UP OR VACCINES FOR EVERY VIRUS ON EARTH.

· CHAPTER SIX ·

DIVERSITY OF THOUGHT

On the evening of May 31, 2009, Air France flight 447 took off from Rio de Janeiro, Brazil, on its way to Paris, France. All was pretty standard, and, nearly four hours into the flight, when they were safely at cruising altitude over the Atlantic Ocean, the captain left the cockpit for a scheduled nap. It was usual for the first officer to oversee the aircraft at this stage when the plane was in autopilot.

Shortly after the captain left, the aircraft's pitol tube—a piece of equipment that detects airspeed—failed, causing the autopilot system to disengage. The first officer took control of the plane, without knowing that the pitol tube was broken and sending him inaccurate data. He tried to make sense of the readings and believed he needed to pull the plane's nose upward. He did just that, and it caused the plane's engines to stall.

But the speed readings were still coming through inaccurately, and the data in the cockpit didn't show that they'd stalled. The first officer believed he still had control of the aircraft. He communicated with his co-first officer, who saw the same data and agreed with his assessment. Together, they formed a belief that, ultimately, proved incorrect. Because one of them thought the data was correct, even though the experience was strange, the other believed it. They each validated the other's beliefs.

The first officer continued trying to pull the plane upward without realizing it was stalled and plummeting toward the ocean. The dashboard continued to display confusing data. The alarm that should've indicated the stall didn't trigger. The two officers couldn't figure out what was happening. They called the pilot in a panic. Within seconds of arriving, the captain assessed that the readings were incorrect. There was a sensor error—it was the only explanation—and the plane had stalled. He knew how to fix it, but they didn't have time. Two minutes and forty-five seconds later, they crashed into the ocean.

All 228 people on board died. It was an awful accident. Two years later, the black box recorders were recovered from the ocean floor and, incredibly, still worked. They told us what happened. From the recordings, we learned that everyone involved in those fatal few minutes tried to save the situation. They all did the best they could with inaccurate information and the effects of groupthink.

Groupthink is a phenomenon that occurs when a bunch of people come together to make decisions based on the same data. Usually, a desire to conform and support each other subconsciously encourages them to reinforce existing opinions without considering alternatives. In this case, one person interpreted the data readings, and the other person in the cockpit, working off the same data points, reinforced the original conclusion. When the captain entered, he arrived with a fresh perspective. He relied on a different set of data—the physical sensations he experienced from the aircraft's movement, the noises he could and couldn't hear, and his greater experience in the air. Without the clouding of the assumptions of groupthink, he came to a different conclusion and determined the sensors were reporting incorrectly. Tragically, it was too late to change the outcome.

In the subsequent accident report, investigators were very clear. The investigation director told the media, "We cannot blame the crew. What we can say is that, most probably, this crew and most crews were not prepared to face such an event." He's right. We can't criticize those in the cockpit for reaching incorrect conclusions when faced with inaccurate data. Nor can we fault them for falling into the trap of groupthink. This common phenomenon plays out in groups of all sizes and all situations, regardless of experience or education. But it is amazing to think that, within seconds, a person outside of the group was able to lean into a different set of data and reach a different conclusion.

GROUPTHINK AT THE OFFICE

The majority of corporate America isn't faced with making split-second, life-or-death decisions for hundreds of people. Thank god. They are, however, plagued by groupthink. It happens within all organizations. Imagine you convene a meeting in your company's conference room to talk about a supply chain issue you've been having. You're done trying to make incremental changes that cause more headaches than they solve. You want to radically rethink the supply process and find a solution that will work for the long term.

So, you gather together all your top-level executives, shut the doors, and ask them to set aside their phones for three damn minutes while you explain the challenges. You tell them about this guy named Jon, who wrote a book about an elephant, and how he says to get radical solutions you need to whiteboard this shit. So that's what you're going to do.

"Let's be really creative here," you say to the assembled team, and you open up the floor for ideas. A few people suggest a few things, and others jump on those suggestions. They talk about things you've tried in the past and ways you could tweak the failed attempts. But there are no unique ideas. No one brings anything new to the table. Trying to extract creative suggestions feels like pulling teeth. And now you think Jon's a dick for promising that whiteboarding stuff works.

I'm not a dick. (Most of the time.) But if this is how it goes down for you, I'm also not surprised. Here is groupthink in action. The chances are good that everyone in that room has a similar background. If it's a company based in Chicago, the room is filled with Chicagoans. They're probably all upper-middle-class people. They all have kids, drive SUVs, and make multiple six-figures a year. Every one of them is college-educated, has worked in the same industry, and has been with the company for about a decade.

They're all working with very similar inputs. They've seen the same things in life. They've had so many shared experiences that they now think almost as one. They're the same. There's no diversity. Their thought patterns are aligned, and it leads to the same old, predictable problem-solving. It's not effective. It's just boring.

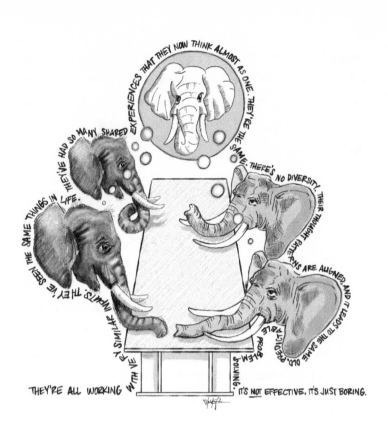

They're all working with very similar inputs. They've seen the same things in life. They've had so many shared experiences that they now think almost as one. They're the same. There's no diversity. Their thought patterns are aligned, and it leads to the same old, predictable problem solving. It's **NOT** effective. It's just boring.

DIVERSE VIEWPOINTS

Imagine bringing diverse viewpoints into that meeting instead. What if every participant brought their own set of life experiences—data points, if you will—from which to be inspired? How would it be different if you brought in an artist from Manhattan, an emergency room doctor from New Orleans, and a taxi driver from Los Angeles? What if you sat them down with your executive team and said, "Hey, let's solve this problem." I mean, you can imagine the crazy shit that would come out of that meeting, right? Some of the suggestions might not work, but you only need one amazing idea.

It's easier and, in many ways, more comfortable to rely on those around you who share your background and viewpoints. It is not more effective, though. Even if you're trying to solve an issue unique to your company, outsiders inevitably have an influence. In the supply chain example, you're likely dealing with suppliers and transportation companies led by people with different priorities and reference points from you. No company is an island, after all.

We all know the value of industry experience and understanding, but we forget the importance of fresh perspectives. If you want to avoid the traps of groupthink, where you can't come up with any new or innovative ideas, you must include people who see the world differently. You must deliberately bring together alternative viewpoints so that you can see new things.

Then, you can solve issues that affect you and others who are not like you. You can have truly successful whiteboarding sessions where you invent innovative solutions. You can have the freedom to think, *Hey, maybe that aircraft's sensor is actually faulty. Perhaps we've stalled.* From life and death situations to boring boardroom meetings, the antidote to groupthink is diversity of thought.

GROWING UP DIVERSE

When we say "diversity," a lot of people think of racial diversity. In the US, just like many other places around the world, race and ethnicity have a major impact on people's life experiences. Unfortunately, we don't yet live in a world where everyone has the same opportunities.

I grew up in an ethnically diverse household, raised by three women of color and a white grandfather and mom. Oddly, I never really thought about it as a child. I saw the women who raised my brother and me had a different skin tone than us. I knew they cooked in a different style than my mom and grandfather. Their meals were Southern, things like incredible greens just drenched in butter. My grandfather always served cabbage. It was good, but it was always the same. Between the skin colors, foods, and various life perspectives, it felt normal to have variety in life.

I know that isn't true for everyone. Perhaps the majority of people find it normal to be surrounded by more of the same: the same skin tone, same food, same language, culture, and beliefs. Maybe that's why some people struggle to accept diversity—to them, it feels so foreign. It's very hard for me to imagine disliking someone based on a variable like skin tone, because I was taught, from an early age, that people of all appearances can be family. For us, family was the people who cared for and loved you. It didn't matter if they were blood relatives or not. If they were there, they were family.

This is very different from how my kids are growing up today. Sadly, we don't have many people left on my side anymore. Helen, Dottie, and Louise have passed away, as have my grandparents and mom. My wife has an incredible extended family, though, which means my kids are surrounded by an awesome group of grandparents, aunts, uncles, and cousins. I'm very grateful for that, and I'm also aware that our extended family isn't a very diverse group. It means my wife and I have to make a deliberate effort to expose our kids to diversity. We take them to restaurants of all ethnicities. We've traveled with them, and plan to take them around the world when we can. As a family, we go to arts festivals that let our kids see different people, art, and interpretations of life. We've taken them to listen to music on Bourbon Street, famous in New Orleans as a vibrant, cultural melting pot, and to Mardi Gras, to experience a unique celebration. We work hard to let them see the world that exists beyond their immediate life.

When I was a kid, though, my family didn't have to make such a deliberate effort to introduce diversity. Every story, every meal, every aspect of every day was influenced by people with profoundly diverse experiences. Growing up with such varied life perspectives taught me there is no singular belief in the way the world works. There is no single right religion or proper way of speaking or best food. Helen, Dottie, and Louise would've argued to their graves that green beans in butter were best, but my grandfather would never have agreed. Knowing that diversity exists taught me to ask questions and seek other people's opinions because I knew they'd be different—and offer more insights—than mine alone.

INCOME DIVERSITY

If we want to solve issues and challenges, unlock opportunities, and radically reimagine the future, we need to consider diversity in all its forms. We need to consider the obvious diversity considerations (Are you black? White? Hispanic? Male? Female?) and those that are less obvious. Different perspectives come from *all* classifications. They include sexual orientation, gender identity, race and ethnicity, religion, culture, language, different physical ability, and political allegiance. I'm sure I've missed many others, and you're welcome to send me angry emails about it.

There's another interesting classification that people often forget: income diversity. It's no more or less important than the others I listed, but I want to talk about it here as it's important to understand. Think about the white dude who grew up in a rural area in an environment of workers making nine bucks an hour. He wants to succeed, and he's determined to make his mark on the world. Now, he'll have a very different perspective to the white dude whose parents were doctors, went to a private high school, an Ivy League college, and now makes $200,000 a year. He also wants to succeed and make his mark on the world, but his varied experiences and perceptions will result in him making very different decisions than the first guy.

The rich white guy might have more in common with an African American colleague who grew up with doctor parents and private schooling, and now has a multi-six-figure salary at the same firm. Race matters, *and* other factors must be considered. In this case, considering income diversity will give you more varied viewpoints than thinking about race alone.

When we search for diversity of thought, we must force ourselves to look beyond labels. We should seek out people who truly offer perspectives unique from our own. Find people with different belief systems formed by different experiences. A genuine drive to include varied people and ideas will serve you better than pencil-whipping "diversity" for the sake of political correctness.

DIVERSE THOUGHT IN ACTION

Let's look at the example of the never-ending public health challenge to encourage more people to eat healthy foods. Healthy foods make for healthier people and, in turn, less strain on the economy. Healthy people take fewer sick days, contribute more to society, and require fewer resources. But raw kale tastes like crap and costs more than a bag of chips, so we all know which food low-income families are more likely to choose. Hell, most high-income families choose chips over healthier alternatives, too.

As those who earn less are hit hardest by health challenges, you often hear people talking about improving access to fresh foods for low-income families. They'll say, "Well, maybe supermarkets can increase consumption of fresh foods for low-income families by providing easy-to-understand menus that show how affordable healthy meals can be." And you probably think the same thing I did. *What a great idea!*

But if the conference room has diversity of thought, there might be someone there who actually understands the low-income community the program needs to reach. They'll say, "Wait, you missed something. People in this community aren't going to the supermarket. They won't even see your glossy menu cards next to the shelf full of kale."

Then, they'll explain that many people in their community don't own a car, so they'd have to take the bus to and from the supermarket, and it's a pain in the ass to carry groceries on public transit. So, they might go there once a month, but they buy most of their food from a corner store. It's the only convenient location. And what food does the corner store sell? Chips. Cookies. Crackers.

With diversity of thought, you can discover that the problem won't be solved with affordable menu cards stacked in the supermarket. And you can make that discovery before you spend a fortune hiring some celebrity chef to design the damn things and printing a billion of them. You can figure out that the solution might be in supplying corner stores with fresh food products, and actually do something that will make an impact.

But you won't get there without diversity of thought. I can guarantee that if you got a bunch of high-net-worth individuals in a room and asked them to solve the challenge of encouraging low-income families to eat fresh foods, you'd end up with some healthy menu bullshit clogging up a retail environment. You'd totally miss the way life works in the communities you're trying to impact.

I know that because *this is a true story*. My wife has done a lot of public health work throughout her career, and she worked with a coalition to pilot this very program in corner stores. They discovered ownership rates for vehicles were low in the communities they were working in, and people were getting their food from corner stores because they were more convenient to access without a car.

I can almost hear you thinking, *I need a research project! I can do that. I'll just buy my diversity of thought*. I've got bad news: a research study alone will not help you. Without innovative ideas to direct your study, you won't get the information you need. Get someone in the room who understands your target audience, or the supply chain, or whatever it is you're trying to solve for, and hold yourself accountable to their diverse viewpoints.

EXPANDING YOUR PERSONAL VIEWPOINT

If you're reading this thinking, *Well, shit. I don't have a diverse or unique viewpoint to bring to the table*, there is hope. First, no one set of life experiences is more or less valuable than anyone else's. Your viewpoint is important. Just make sure it's not the only one in the room. Second, you can expand your own viewpoint, no matter how sheltered your life has been until now.

Howard Schultz is a great example of someone who deliberately expanded his experiences and built a business on diversity of thought. That business was Starbucks, which we all know for its almost-guaranteed presence in our communities.

In 1982, when Schultz joined Starbucks as director of retail operations and marketing, coffee meant something very different to Americans. Back then, it was a commodity you paid fifty cents for at a diner. A small step above water, it had usually been sitting in a pot for hours and carried a faint burnt taste.

A year later, Starbucks sent Schultz to Italy for a research trip. He fell in love with the way Italian culture used coffee as a conversation starter. Cafes were meeting points. They had rich, dynamic atmospheres and were places of community and enjoyment. By looking at diverse populations and taking time to understand the Italian approach to coffee, he unlocked the potential of Starbucks. He took a circuitous path; he went home and founded another coffee company that eventually bought Starbucks and its name. Through the journey, though, he created not just another cheap commodity, but a true community asset focused around a premium coffee experience.

Imagine if, back in the seventies, Schultz had filled a room with people from middle America and said, "Okay, let's dream big. What could coffee be?" No one would have imagined the concept of Starbucks as we know it today. You can imagine a focus group coming up with different flavors of instant coffee and bulk-buy discounts. But if you only know coffee as a cheap, commoditized entity, that's all you imagine it to be. Instead, Schultz took himself outside of the world he knew. He sought out another viewpoint. He learned from and was inspired by new and exciting experiences. And now he's a billionaire.

Of course, I'm not suggesting Schultz's fortune is entirely thanks to diversity of thought. Any major success is the result of a million moving parts. We know, though, that

Starbucks went on to shatter expectations of what coffee could be in the US. It now has more than thirty thousand stores in over seventy countries. It elevated the industry in the US and overseas.

You can argue the good and bad of the variables within the company, but on the whole, it's also become a positive meeting point in most communities. Every Friday morning, I go to my local Starbucks, which is near one of the top public high schools in New Orleans. There are usually forty or so kids in there, hanging out before class starts. Think about that for a moment. There aren't a lot of positive, safe, clean places for teenagers to hang out. But Starbucks provides that. And I know my local store is not the only one offering a safe meeting space for all kinds of people.

You have to expand your own diversity of thought. The only way to create new output is to start with fresh input. If you want new, innovative, exciting ideas that will lead to a fulfilling life, you must start with new experiences. Otherwise, you'll just keep regurgitating the same old fifty-cent, stale, burnt coffee.

SURROUNDING YOURSELF WITH DIFFERENT VIEWPOINTS

Once Schultz was inspired by Italian coffee culture, he surrounded himself with people who understood its magic. With their help, he successfully brought a diverse approach to coffee in the US. No one can be innovative entirely on their own. The people you surround yourself with matter. So how do you bring diverse viewpoints into your business or organization?

At GE, we actually brought in the artist from Manhattan, the emergency room doctor from New Orleans, and the taxi driver from Los Angeles. We did think tanks with people from intentionally diverse backgrounds. That was easy at GE, where we had money to spend on stuff like that. Most companies don't have budgets for crazy whiteboarding meetings with all sorts of random people from across the country.

You can find diversity within your organization, though. If you want to solve a sales challenge, consult with different groups within your company. Bring in your accounting team lead and the HR benefits coordinator. Ask someone outside of your project group. Look for diversity of thought, and you will find it.

That said, the broader the level of diversity, the better your outcomes. If you're in a leadership position, you should hire based on diversity of thought. This was *not* how GE generally hired. They had a list of business schools where they went graduate-hunting each spring. A recruiter would visit college campuses identifying the high-achievers and luring them into the company. Many other businesses follow this practice, and *it is insane.*

Schools don't change. Year after year, the same type of student is accepted into the same school. In business classes, the same old faculty members teach the same bullshit case studies over and over again. When companies hire new graduates, they inherit the same experiences and thinking patterns. This doesn't do anyone any good. Obviously, certain jobs require certain skill sets, but employers can solve that. A lifetime of unique experiences cannot be so easily taught.

I was lucky to get into GE, as I went to Louisiana State University, which was not one of their regular recruiting schools. But I happened to meet an officer of the company who took a liking to me. I had a different background than most of my GE peers, and I think that benefited them and me. In part, it gave me a fresh take on what to look for when hiring my own teams.

In job interviews, I'd get a sense of someone's experience and viewpoint by asking them to walk me through their background. I ask candidates what they loved and hated in high school. I ask what was challenging and what felt easy. I ask how they chose which college to apply to and what they loved about their time there. I find out what makes them happy. This encourages people to share the experiences that informed their way of thinking today. It helps me figure out if their viewpoint differs from mine.

Take the person who says they loved college because they

attended their parents' alma mater and were the star athlete there. Compare them to someone who says they struggled in college because they were on their own. They were always tired because they worked long hours on the side to pay for their tuition. You can *feel* the difference between those two responses. Neither is better than the other. They just reveal details that let you assess which person will best round out your team, so you don't have a bunch of employees who look the same, act the same, and think the same.

Groupthink in your business might not be as devastating as the Air France disaster, but it will prevent you from breaking free and making leaps forward. And increasing diversity in your business isn't just a nice thing to do; it will result in more imaginative and more fulfilling business leaps. It's truly transformational for individuals and businesses. Of course, it's not enough to just bring in a token minority guy; when you introduce diversity of thought, you must create an ecosystem in which it can thrive.

CHAPTER SEVEN

AN ECOSYSTEM OF KINDNESS

I've been in meetings that are derailed by hate. I mean, we're talking about corporate America, so this doesn't usually mean screaming matches or iPhones being thrown across the conference room. I'm talking about those meetings where a leader cannot see past their dislike for a team member, so they refuse to listen to their ideas. The team member could say, "I have an idea that'll make us $1 billion," and the leader just won't hear it. They can't get past their hatred to assess the idea objectively. So, they talk over the team member, or shut them down, or even humiliate them in some snide way. Personal opinions and feelings get in the way of business decisions. It happens every day, and it's terrible.

I've also been in meetings where great ideas are killed

because they didn't meet a certain profitability threshold, time constraint, or some other shortsighted variable. Anything that doesn't align with these arbitrary numbers is instantly dismissed. And it's the dismissals that are often unkind. I've heard leaders say, "Eff off. That idea won't meet our profitability threshold. It won't work. Get out of here." You get these really contentious strategy reviews and project discussions that lack any empathy, kindness, or even simple politeness.

What happens when an employee is shut down in that way, either because the boss can't stand them or because their idea is deemed stupid? Most of the time, they think, *Screw it. I'm not going to pitch new ideas anymore. We can just continue delivering in the same old way, and I won't try and change anything.* They lose morale, shut down, and stop performing. They don't contribute anymore. They don't bother to innovate. And I don't blame them.

BUILDING A BASE OF SUPPORTERS

When you're trying to do something new and innovative, you need people around you to participate. That might mean they lobby for your ideas, offer encouragement, or lend their efforts to your goal. This isn't just useful. It's *essential.* Whether you're in a big company like GE, where there's a natural friction that slows movement, or in a smaller environment where resources are limited, you need a fan base of supporters for yourself and your cause. When people are championing your effort, you'll have more help. You'll feel more confident. You'll be encouraged to keep pushing, even when it feels hard. Supporters increase your probability of success.

Think of supporters as a personal board of advisors that provides unique perspectives, advice, and guidance. The more you can build out a diverse board of advisors, the better. As this is an informal congregation, it relies on kindness. You need others to kindly donate their time, energy, and insights to your cause. To encourage this, you must be kind to them; no one will willingly help a jackass.

So, it might sound soft and fluffy, but the hard fact is that innovative ideas are more likely to succeed when created within an ecosystem of kindness. And let's face it, you should practice kindness on a day-to-day basis anyway. There's no need to be the person whom everyone hates.

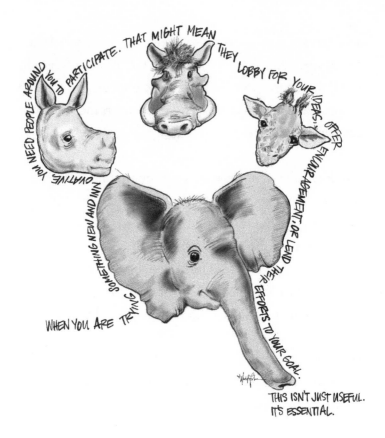

YOU NEED PEOPLE AROUND YOU TO PARTICIPATE. THAT MIGHT MEAN THEY LOBBY FOR YOUR IDEAS, OFFER ENCOURAGEMENT, OR LEND THEIR EFFORTS TO YOUR GOAL. WHEN YOU ARE TRYING SOMETHING NEW AND INNOVATIVE

THIS ISN'T JUST USEFUL. IT'S ESSENTIAL.

FINDING PEOPLE WHO ARE KIND

An ecosystem of kindness works in two directions. You need to be kind, and you need to surround yourself with others who are kind. To do the latter, you need to look for individuals who believe in noble intent. By that, I mean people who assume those around them intend to do good—even if it doesn't feel great when you're on the receiving end of their actions.

Sometimes you can sense if a person believes in noble intent. They just give off a good vibe. Other times, you need to ask outright: *Do you think people in business often do things just for individual success instead of the good of the company? Would you say this industry requires a win-at-all-costs attitude?* If someone nods in response and tells you most businesspeople are singularly driven by money, that shows they're a skeptic. If they shake their head and say, "No, I think most people try to do good because they know it's the right thing," well, that tells a different story. That's a person who trusts others will try to act for the right reasons. They're not a cynic. They believe in doing things for a greater purpose. For someone like this, business isn't just about making a profit; they care about doing meaningful work in the world. This is someone who won't just go through the motions but will work with purpose, with a mission, to solve problems. It's someone you want on your team.

Skepticism translates to negativity; trust turns into cheerleading. You don't want skeptics shitting on your innovative new ideas. They turn up to meetings with their own agendas, ready to dismiss your ideas the moment you make a mistake. No, you want a cheerleader who will trust that even if your plan sounds stupid, you're trying your best to improve the world. You want someone who won't shoot you down if you screw up on the journey. Because if you're making big leaps and doing new things, you won't get it right 100 percent of the time.

This isn't a huge how-to guide on detecting kindness, because when you know to look for it, it's easy to spot. We've been looking for kindness since the first day of elementary school, trying to make friends with someone who wouldn't be a bully. You know how to do this. But remember to look in more than one place. Your ecosystem of kindness can come from a professional workplace group, an informal network of friends and colleagues, or a combination. Make it a diverse bunch of people who will encourage you to imagine change that really makes an impact.

If you can't find an ecosystem of kindness at work, that's a red flag. You should probably start looking for another job. I'm not joking. Without kindness, no one will want to be there. Good employees will eventually leave, the company's value will erode, and the place won't last for long. Plus, life is short, right? You have a choice of where to spend your days. Do you really want to devote your time and effort to a place that sucks? Cut your losses and get out.

Now, if you're the CEO of a company that's not kind, you can't just cut and run. Instead, start by asking yourself some hard questions. Are you part of the problem? Why are you running a business that way? What opportunities are you missing because people can't raise their hands and talk about things that are broken? How could you encourage good people to contribute their best work? These aren't easy questions to answer, and it won't be a fast road to recovery. They'll trigger more observations and paths for exploration. Your business is worth the effort, though.

BUSINESS IS THE PLACE FOR THIS

If you still think business isn't the place for kindness, I want to *kindly* remind you that you are not a robot. You're a human. You have the capability to be productive, business-like, *and* kind—if you so choose. These are not exclusive attributes. Every day, you can choose to deliver news, good or bad, with kindness or like a cold-hearted douchebag. You can choose to frame your criticisms in a kind way. Or not. You can choose how you interact with others and, in turn, affect the way they support—or don't support—you. This doesn't mean you avoid giving criticism, discipline, or worse when needed. You just choose to deliver it with kindness.

When we prepared to transition Big Ass Fans to the new owners, we had to lay some people off. And if you were one of them, you might be sitting there thinking, *Jon isn't kind. He fired me. I don't have a job because of him.* Yeah. That sucks. The reality is that, sometimes, you need to make tough business decisions.

These can still be executed with kindness. But that's not how I did it at Big Ass Fans. At the time, I was focused on getting the job done, being discreet, and pleasing stake-holders. Juggling all those balls, it felt like I was in a difficult position. It was infinitely worse for those I laid off. I got caught up in my own bullshit and didn't offer as much kindness as I should have to the employees who were most affected.

I know I didn't behave that well because the remaining staff kicked my butt in subsequent town hall meetings. Figuratively, I mean. We were still civilized human beings. After the lay-offs, I started to realize we needed to be more communicative and talk through the restructuring with those who were left, so I scheduled a bunch of town hall meetings. I invited about thirty employees to each session, and I used the time to listen to their concerns, experiences, and questions. I think I got in front of every single employee in some format. I gave them context for the restructuring and some transparency around the circumstances that led to it.

The staff was still pissed that their friends had been let go and that they hadn't been spoken to sooner, but those meetings were vital in getting them on board with the company's new direction. They also kind of sucked. I could feel the staff's negative energy. I could see it in their body language. I heard mutterings of people looking for other jobs because they didn't feel theirs was safe. It wasn't much fun to be around all that, but I learned a lot.

It showed me how easy it is to derail an organization when you don't operate with kindness. And it taught me how much can be recovered by leaning into kindness—because things did start to improve. As I kept showing up with transparency, honestly sharing the context of our challenges, the staff softened toward me. They thanked me for sharing the context of their colleagues' lay-offs, even though it was after the fact. I'd bump into someone in line at Starbucks, and they'd say they appreciated the effort I'd put into transitioning the company. I treated them with kindness, and they responded *in kind*.

It showed me that you could go through terrible situations like downsizing and manage it with kindness. You can hold people accountable and do it with kindness. You can have strict guidelines and metrics and outlandish goals and follow them with kindness. You can even screw up, be the biggest asshole imaginable, and recover with kindness. Business is not always easy, but the kinder we are, the more we create environments that thrive, regardless of the pressures they're under.

YOU DON'T NEED PERMISSION TO BE KIND

We each choose who we want to be and how we'll act in life. I can yammer on about how you should be consistently kind, but no one is going to stand over you at work, waving a kind wand, magically making you say nice things to people. Nor are there any Kind Police patrolling meetings rooms, handing out tickets to anyone being an asshole.

You need to enforce this yourself. You need to monitor your own behavior.

That doesn't mean you have to go it alone. You could literally ask someone at the office if you're being kind. Enlist anyone you can trust to tell you the truth. My wife helps keep me accountable. She'll occasionally say, "Hey, you're not being that kind right now." Or she might use less kind language. However she says it, it's an area I need her help to improve on, so I'm incredibly grateful for her assistance.

Whichever way you find to get help, the responsibility remains on you to make it happen. You need to find a way to create an ecosystem of kindness. Then, those around you will champion your cause, innovate on your behalf, and encourage you in your efforts. With that in place, you'll have no excuse to stay chained up.

CHAPTER EIGHT

PERMISSION TO BREAK FREE

When my grandmother fled Belarus, there was no mandatory evacuation notice. The government did not order anyone to leave. There was a lot of uncertainty, and many people were choosing to wait and see what would happen. There were a lot of rumors, but no one knew the Germans would invade the country, or that they'd ultimately kill more than one million Belarusians over their three-year occupation.

Without any directives from government, my grandmother analyzed the environment and the variables at play. She interpreted the data coming in from newspapers and the community gossip mill and formed a personal conviction that her family would be safest away from everything they knew. Without being sure of the future of Belarus, she bet her life on a long and dangerous journey to a strange land. When she eventually arrived in the US, there was no welcome guidebook for illegal immigrants escaping the Nazis. She had to figure out for herself how to do life in his new world. That's incredibly compelling. I wonder if I would've been that brave and resourceful.

Most people in modern America operate in a very different way than my grandmother. They won't move unless a governing body directs them. They wait for permission then react to instruction. We see this dynamic playing out with real threats all the time. I mean, thankfully, the Nazis aren't knocking at America's door, but think about, for example, hurricane season.

When a hurricane approaches a city, often the mayor will look at the variables, interpret the data, ask some other people when she realizes she doesn't understand the data, then declare a mandatory evacuation. With this newfangled thing called the internet, most citizens have access to the same data and analysis tools as the mayor. Even those who aren't down with the internet may look out the window and see a big-ass storm brewing. But do they leave before the evacuation notice comes? No. Almost everyone stays put until they're ordered to move.

Now, I'm not advising that everyone should abandon hurricane areas before authorities ask them. I just think it's fascinating that most folks who live in hurricane zones know what these storms can do, yet they don't take it on *themselves* to decide if and when to evacuate. They wait for permission or orders from authorities.

THE HABIT OF HIERARCHICAL THINKING

This happens in corporate America, too. People don't usually like to take action unless given permission by their boss. In a lot of big companies, employees find themselves sitting back and waiting for the new corporate agenda to be pushed down from the top. Only then will they react to the instructions and start slowly shifting forward. They take incremental steps as far as they feel able, before waiting for more guidance from above. This is the habit of hierarchical thinking. It's a system that doesn't set anyone up to create a lasting impact. It just shuffles employees down a well-trod path no faster than the boss will allow.

Here's the truth: big-time executives make a shitload of money. And when they make a shitload of money, they want to continue making a shitload of money. So, there are no incentives for them to add risk to their organization. Zero. That means they're just not interested in trying new, innovative ideas. They're too busy focusing on the next quarter. They're set up with shortsighted procedures, processes, and goals that keep them comfortably ticking over from one reporting period to the next.

This isn't because they're lousy people; it's simply a reflection of the money-risk dynamic. I imagine what I'd do if I was hired into SC Johnson or some other big cleaning company and handed $5 million a year to run the company. Even with all my high-flying beliefs, I know I'd have a hard time, psychologically, taking risks with the business. Leaders in those positions are paid to keep companies on an incremental upward trajectory, not to rock the boat. There's just no incentive to take risks.

Imagine, though, if a CEO was paid based on the future success of an organization instead of the bullshit stock price at the end of the quarter. Imagine if they were paid a dollar today but, in ten years, if the company is super-successful, they get paid big-time. How differently would they think? This is, incidentally, how Elon Musk is reportedly paid by Tesla. His annual salary is apparently $1, with the rest of his compensation awarded in stock and performance-based bonuses, at least some of which are only available once Tesla's market value rises above a certain threshold. Leaders will only take innovative leaps when performance is the greater motivator.

If it's futile to wait for the boss to grant permission for you to innovate, experiment, and break free of the normal way of things, then you must give yourself permission. If you are the boss, you need to stop holding out for someone else—shareholders, the board of directors, your direct reports—to give you permission. This has to come from you.

How do you summon the courage to break free of their expectations? You start by accepting you have the capacity to effect change. Then you tug on the chain and take small steps to build your confidence. You identify the impact you want to make and imagine how you'll create change. You surround yourself with diversity of thought and an ecosystem of kindness. Then, you actually have to do the damn work. But you won't make progress on anything if you're busy playing Monday Morning Quarterback.

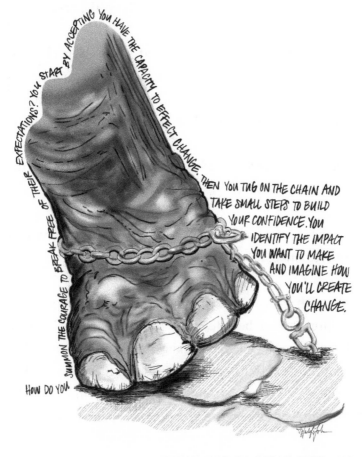

MONDAY MORNING QUARTERBACK

Imagine you're a guy born and raised in Massachusetts, who lived all over the country before finally settling in New Orleans. You worked for a big business for many years, made a name for yourself restructuring and selling a midsized company, and have now founded a cleaning products brand. You work hard all week with your business partner, and at the weekends, you throw a football with your kids, make some good meals, and watch the New Orleans Saints kick ass on the football field (or occasionally get their ass kicked).

Then Monday morning rolls around. When you get into the office, you and your business partner kick off your weekly meeting with a good ol' recap of Sunday's game. You sit with your coffees and dissect all the quarterback's shitty moves.

"Did you see at the end of the third? He should have run the ball there," you say.

"Yeah, and after that, why didn't he pass?" says your partner. You're both playing Monday Morning Quarterback.

This is the game where you make yourself feel superior by pointing out all the defects of a decision. I know. I've done it. But you—and me—are making these assertions based on *known data*. After the game, you know the outcome. You understand it was a bad move to pass the ball in a particular moment because you've seen what happened.

There's nothing special in sitting around talking about what a quarterback should or should not have done. The magic is in assessing those decisions in real time. That's why NFL players get paid the big bucks. They have to watch the defense, call the plays, work with the coaches, and make decisions in the middle of a fast-paced game, all while strong-as-nails opponents come running, trying to knock them down.

In business, you can be one of two people: the real-deal quarterback or the Monday morning quarterback. You can run fast, push innovative ideas forward, drive change, and rally others. Or you can sit back, wait for things to happen around you, then talk about how you would've done things differently.

The world does not need more Monday morning quarterbacks. We don't benefit from people who are comfortable criticizing others' efforts without trying anything themselves. That's not helpful for anyone. It just makes you kind of a jerk. And we've already done the chapter on kindness, so you know why that's bad.

We need more real-deal quarterbacks willing to take risks in the moment. We need people who will support and celebrate others who take risks. God knows, entrepreneurs and businesses who try new things get criticized enough in the media without being surrounded by critics in their network. Our company, Truman's, is working hard to do good things in the world, and we get criticized all the time. Trolls on Twitter tell us they would've chosen different materials for the reusable bottles and give us shit for shipping product direct to consumer instead of getting on the shelves at Walmart.

If I was surrounded in my personal and work life by people who also questioned my every move, I think I'd have quit the game long ago. Criticism fuels risk aversion. Deep down, we all want to be accepted and supported, and when that doesn't happen, instinct kicks in and sends us running back to the safety of the same old thing.

Once you've decided to do something interesting, innovative, unknown, and risky, ditch the Monday morning quarterback attitude. It's not pretty. Stop criticizing others and surround yourself with other real-deal quarterbacks willing to play for you.

REWIRING YOURSELF

Unfortunately, it's not enough just to ditch the shitty attitude. You can't just stop criticizing and go quiet. If you want to make a change, you then need to step out of your comfortable little box. That requires a bit of rewiring.

People do not like to be outliers. They feel safer falling into the same box as everyone else than standing alone and cold outside of it. We don't need to get into the psychology of it all—even if you, personally, have a higher tolerance for being an outlier, you know this is generally true. Most people are wired to stay in Belarus. They hunker down when the hurricane comes.

You need to rewire yourself to get comfortable being the outsider, though, because I can tell you what will happen. You'll come up with a great idea at work. It's creative and innovative and all-around awesome. You know no one will give you permission to do this new thing, but you have what you need to execute on it, so you don't bother wasting time waiting for approval. You just step outside the box and get this shit moving.

Then the group down the hall get wind of what you're doing. They sit back and watch, then talk about how they'd have done it differently, if it were up to them. And had someone asked them to run your project, they probably would've done it. But without permission, it never occurred to anyone in that group. They didn't get permission, so they didn't step outside the box. Where does that leave them? Inside! From in there, all they can really do is gossip about you on the outside. And they might not even hide it.

I can't tell you how many meetings I've been in where the only purpose seemed to be to shit on someone's idea. I'm not kidding. I've sat at a conference table, looked at the five people across from me, and thought, *All you know how to do is tell us an idea is terrible*. Because I'd never heard them say anything was positive.

It will feel uncomfortable knowing they're all in their cozy box, talking smack about you and your foolish ideas. Or to sit across from them in a meeting, trying not to get discouraged when they railroad your idea. This is the point where you might think, *This is too hard. I'll just become one of them*. If you are okay with the discomfort, though, you might just be able to push through. You might think, *I've had enough. I'm going to break free of this slow-moving, backwards, risk-averse culture that does everything wrong every day of the fucking week*.

That might sound extreme—or not, if you've been there—but that's a rewired thought. That's how it looks to not care you're outside the box. That's the attitude that will set you free.

READY FOR ACTION

I often wonder how many people working for Windex have those thoughts. In the cleaning products industry, Windex is a major player. You probably have one of their twenty billion types of glass cleaner under your kitchen sink.

I bet there are people working at Windex who know it

doesn't make sense to ship bottles filled with water. But there are probably thousands of—what would you call them...Windexians?—who look at the huge factory filling bottles and think, *This is the way we've always done it. Our customers* want *the product this way. Look how stupid that Truman's company is. It'll never work, selling concentrates like that.* I imagine the poor Windexians who do want to innovate feeling frustrated. I bet they wish big companies weren't so stuck in their ways. Hopefully, this book will inspire them to do something great within Windex or leave and do it great somewhere else.

But they, and anyone else who wants to do great things, must be *ready* to take action. I talk to a lot of people about change, and I ask, "Are you actually ready to break free?" For many, the honest answer is, "Not yet." Had I not grown up with women who convinced me anything was possible, if I hadn't used that courage to take small steps in my early career, I know I also wouldn't be ready to take big leaps today.

But I hope by now you understand that doing nothing is not an option. Things might be comfortable in your bubble, but if you look out the window, you'll see trends all around us that are not positive. Think of the trends toward more pollution, more widespread public health problems, more school shootings, pandemics, homelessness, and horribly divisive politics. They all have the potential to leave the world in a worse place for our kids, even if we provide all we can for them. I suppose you can choose to do nothing, but you will not feel fulfilled. You won't find the peace in knowing you played your part to make the world a better place.

So, if your answer is, "No, I'm not ready to do something radical yet," then start with something small. Go back to wearing red socks with a gray suit. Do what you need to gather your strength and conviction. Then come back to this and know that *you do not need permission* to break free of the chains around your leg. It doesn't matter if your boss, board of directors, or shareholders expect something small and boring from you. Don't wait for them to ask what matters to you. Speak up. Share your conviction. Articulate why your chosen mission is important. Insist they let you act crazy.

If, after all that, your progress is purposefully blocked, then you need to find another outlet for change. That's my polite way of telling you to quit your job. Leave the soul-sucking company. Find somewhere else that will support your goals or create a company of your own. It might sound drastic, but this is about more than waiting for permission. It's your duty to constantly seek things that fulfill you. You are the only person you absolutely must answer to. You're the only one you can act for. My grandmother made decisions for herself as an individual. It's not a stretch to say that saved her life. You must make your decisions, too. And if you want to do good, you have to *do something.*

CHAPTER NINE

CREATING AN INSPIRED LEGACY

I didn't grow up eating Indian food. It wasn't until I was an adult that I realized I *loved* it. My wife and I were in San Francisco staying with friends of Indian descent. We went out every day exploring the city and returned to their house every evening exhausted. There, they poured us a glass of wine and served the most phenomenal Indian meals. One evening, after finishing every scrap of food on my plate, I put down my fork and said, "Oh my god, Sarita. I need to know how to do this." Sarita laughed and said, "Oh, you just throw some of this in there, some of that," and she listed off a bunch of spices.

I've never been intimidated in the kitchen. I love to cook, and I'll give any recipe a try. So, I went home and tried to recreate the Indian meals every night. I had Sarita's list of ingredients and basic instructions, but I didn't really know what I was doing. I didn't understand how to develop all those complex, intense flavors Indian food is famous for.

The first meal was...not great. The spices were overwhelmingly bitter. It had a weird, lumpy consistency. My wife didn't want it and, I had to admit, neither did I. We threw it out and ate a pizza. Now, I don't like to fail at anything, so the next night, I tried again. This time, the spices weren't strong enough. It was oily and gross and not remotely close to Sarita's incredible creations. I was determined to figure it out, though. The following day, I thought, *I've got this*. I did not. I tried again and again, every evening for two solid weeks. (This was in our pre-kid life, when I had time to indulge in culinary insanity.)

Finally, my wife cornered me in the kitchen.

"Look, Jon, I love it when you cook," she said. "You're a great cook! Your roasted Brussel sprouts are awesome. But you cannot figure this out. These meals are awful. We're wasting so much food. Can we just order Indian?" She was right. We placed a take-out order at a local restaurant called Kashmir, and I gave up on the mission.

I've made some complex meals in my life. I once nailed an African peanut butter stew that was incredible, if I say so myself. But for some reason, these Indian meals kicked my ass. It was the biggest kitchen mess of my life. I hate to fail, so this hurt a bit, but I'm still so glad I tried. For me, cooking represents so much more than just feeding yourself. It's about the colors, the smells, the variety of ingredients, and experimenting with new things. I experiment with the old, too, creating meals my ancestors used to make.

These days, it's all about creating a wonderful meal and experience for my kids. My wife introduced an idea to our dinners called "Rose, Bud, Thorn" inspired by some good friends. We go around the table and say what our favorite part of the day was (that's the rose), what we're looking forward to tomorrow (the bud), and what irritated us today (the thorn). It sounds a bit cheesy, but it's a really nice way to come together over a good meal and share our experiences. Trying new foods, restaurants, and ways of cooking is all part of that.

In experiencing new things, I'm inspired to solve problems in new ways. This is true for the kitchen and the conference room. Great cooking, meaningful moments with the family, and exciting work contributions all require you to be present and engaged. New ideas are unlocked when you're tuned-in and experiencing different things. Your mind opens to possibilities you hadn't before considered— or perhaps even known existed. You ask questions when confronted with things you don't know well, and both the act of inquiring and the answers themselves can inspire you.

When I discovered that I can't cook Indian food, it reminded me there are just some things that other people are better at. As we looked at what Truman's could be, we saw there were other small operations already creating excellent concentrate cleaning components but without the capacity to package, sell, and distribute them to the public. At the time, I didn't know much about chemical compounds and reactions and the ingredients required to cut through grease marks on a kitchen countertop. But these people knew what they were doing.

Instead of getting our asses kicked trying something we weren't good at—chemistry—we partnered with an incredible company that was already skilled at mixing cleaning chemicals. We brought our skills in business, supply chains, operations, and sales and together made Truman's a reality.

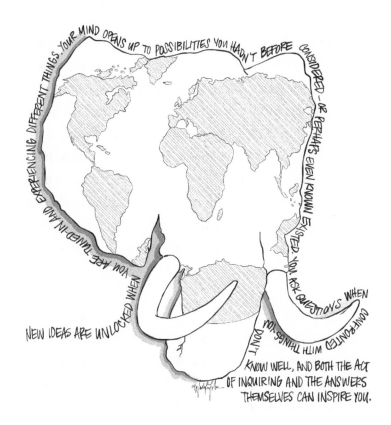

SOMETHING NEW

I want you to be open-minded to change. Be willing to take ideas that inspire you to the environment they need to thrive—even if that requires drastic changes. The unfortunate truth is that not every environment allows for the kind of leaps we've discussed. Some workplaces won't tolerate you doing your own thing without permission or won't provide the support you need to pursue your innovative ideas.

Deep down, you already know if your current situation will allow for the changes you need to make. When you look at the people in your office, you can tell if they're hungry to hear new ideas. You can sense how they'll react when you present an innovative suggestion. You know if they'll ask to hear more or tell you all the reasons it won't work. If it's the latter, it's time to look outside your current organization. You can try and fix the culture, but do you really believe it will change? You have a better chance of making an impact elsewhere than of revolutionizing an existing company's culture on your own.

I don't care what industry you're in; there are a lot of companies doing similar things to yours but with a different philosophy. If you make mattresses, you can find another mattress company that looks at the world in a different way. There's a mattress firm out there trying to use less impactful materials, trying to shrink the emissions involved in the supply chain, trying to provide free beds to foster kids. I don't know which companies they are, but I'll bet my Brussel sprout recipe they exist. If the desire is there, you can find your match. You can join a place that shares your goals.

Alternatively, if you're willing to take on the risk, you can start your own company. There is risk involved in that, and I don't want to pretend otherwise. And it's not like you'll be independent of all influence. At Truman's, we went out and raised capital to help us continue to grow. Now, we're somewhat influenced by the knowledge that others are invested in our success. For us, that is worth it, though. We've created a company based on what we believe is important, and we're making a real difference in the world.

We also, let's face it, had a good financial cushion after leaving Big Ass Fans. That made it easier to take the risk than if we were, say, struggling to pay off college loans or wrangling a big mortgage. If you're trying to support four young kids in an expensive neighborhood and only just making ends meet, maybe you don't want the financial risk of your own business. That's okay. Just be honest with yourself and refuse to let it become an excuse for inaction.

Find another way to step forward. Get funding—there are people who are willing to invest in great ideas. Find a company that'll pay you a set salary every month *and* let you work toward your goals. There's no filter that says you cannot become an entrepreneur, or you will not find another job. Regardless of your situation, regardless of the economy or politics or anything else, *there is always a way*.

KEEP YOURSELF ACCOUNTABLE

I don't suggest these moves lightly. Leaving a company you've committed your time and energy to is a big move, but you can't make big leaps without big movement. So, hold yourself accountable to your desire to do more. Say you decide to talk to your leadership team because you believe they'll be willing to accept your innovative ideas. If three months go by and you haven't scheduled that meeting, that's a problem. Hold yourself accountable by taking the required actions. Send the email. Schedule the meeting to share your ideas. Write notes on what you'll present. Make it happen.

If six months go by and you still haven't taken any action, it's probably because your environment doesn't really encourage innovation. It feels too risky to take this step. It's easier to focus on all the other things that come across your desk. Then, you need to decide if you really want things to be different. Accept your answer, commit to it, and take action.

You don't need to waltz into the Monday morning meeting, throw your middle fingers up, tell everyone there they're assholes, and smash the printer on your way out. I mean, you can. The printer probably deserves it. It might be more effective, though, to start with steps toward breaking free. Work on your resume. Meet with people connected to a company you'd like to work with. Build your public profile to get your name out there and become recognized by those you want to connect with.

If a month, two months, three months go by and you can't point to any actions you've taken, then you're not moving anywhere. You're stuck. You're lost in the moment. Again. If you don't *take action*, five years will go past and you'll still be sitting at your desk feeling like shit.

Get re-inspired. Read this book again. Cook a new recipe (probably not Indian). Spend time in new areas of your industry. Visit the factory floor or have coffee with someone in another department. Try new things, get inspired again, and re-commit to taking action. Go to another company or start your own entrepreneurial endeavor, but don't waste more time staying stuck.

STEPPING INTO LEAPS

Alex, my business partner, and I were lucky to be in a slightly different position when we started Truman's. We'd exited Big Ass Fans as part of the company's sale and were looking for what to do next. Leaping into an entrepreneurial endeavor still required a big dose of guts.

The easy path would've been to become a business consultant. Believe me—enough people have asked, "Why didn't you just go into consulting?" It's clear that was the path the world expected of me. But I'd decided to break free of those expectations and do something innovative to change the world. So, I had to actually do the damn thing.

One day, Alex and I sat down in our local Starbucks and said,

"Okay, if we're going to do this, what are the steps to make it real?" We didn't create a drawn-out, boring business plan, but we captured the steps involved into a basic framework. Then we took the first of those steps. Then the next. And before we knew it, we had the supply chain set up. Then we had a website built. Then our first customer. (That was pretty amazing.)

Every time things felt big or overwhelming, I remembered my grandparents. They were willing to risk it all. Their story isn't unique, either. I think of the amazing accountant we use at Truman's. This woman is the founder and CEO of the accounting firm we work with. She's originally from Iran, and when she was little, her parents decided to leave *everything* behind to move them to the US. You hear stories like this everywhere.

The risk of starting a new business looks ridiculous by comparison. Sure, I could lose the money I've invested. I could feel like an idiot if everything fails. It's not exactly the same thing, though, as risking your life and everything you own for your and your children's safety. My ancestors, and the ancestors of all Americans, show us it's possible to step into bigger leaps than we imagine.

CONCLUSION

MAKE YOUR MARK ON THE WORLD

You know what I find most interesting about the moment Neil Armstrong first stepped on the moon? It's not the technology or the science, although that was pretty impressive. I'm fascinated by the reactions of people on earth. I think about the millions of people huddled around their televisions for that iconic moment, together celebrating a giant leap for mankind. In that moment, they reveled in the forward movement of humanity.

These days, we're somewhat numb to big leaps. The world has progressed ever faster, and now we just expect that rockets will go into space, innovations will be made, and someone else will take care of it all. We're no longer in a space race. We're not racing anywhere. With rare exceptions, we find ourselves with no sense of urgency.

Most of the time, we're not considering what our great-great-great-grandkids will think of us. We're just content to go through life, providing just for our kids' direct needs, and not looking beyond that. I think our ancestors saw things differently. They did consider their impact on future generations. They thought about the rich, multilayered concepts of family and community, and of helping those outside of their four walls. They wanted their world to be a significantly better place. They cherished forward progress. We must cherish it, too.

STAND AND RALLY

Any organization is merely the sum of its people. It's the collective thoughts and efforts of those involved. The more people who rally around these ideas, the more people who stand up and lead the charge, the faster our companies—and our world—will move forward. That's an exciting idea. We need executives to raise their hands and say, "I'm going to break free from the normal bullshit. I'm going to do the right thing, and I'm going to take my organization with me." This is how we'll make a change. This is how we'll become a catalyst of change in others.

And we need change. Every day the world faces new and growing macro issues, like new illnesses plaguing the world, or another school shooting, or more icebergs melting. We will continue to face issue after issue after issue, and they will continue to worsen if we don't take action to solve them. We can solve them. We have always improved on health challenges, solved global issues, and used new ideas and information to look at issues in new ways. This is an age-old human trait.

We can bring this attitude into the modern age. We know more now than we did decades ago, years ago, even days ago. In the past, we made some bad decisions about the materials we use. We thought lead wasn't poisonous and asbestos was a miracle material. We thought it didn't matter that we pumped pollution into the waterways. We assumed a solid paycheck was enough to make a person feel fulfilled.

We know better now. So, with our new understanding of the effects we have on our world, let's stand up and make a change. We can use the variables we now know about and harness the information we have. We can build off of new technology to address problems that feel overwhelming. We can move forward, and we should move forward. Because, do you really believe this is the best it can be? Do you think the world can't possibly be any better? I believe it can. Let's solve the issues in the world and, at the same time, leave a legacy for ourselves.

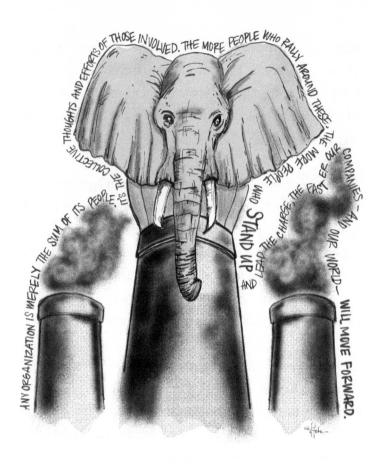

ANY ORGANIZATION IS MERELY THE SUM OF ITS PEOPLE. IT'S THE COLLECTIVE THOUGHTS AND EFFORTS OF THOSE INVOLVED. THE MORE PEOPLE WHO RALLY AROUND THESE. THE MORE PEOPLE WHO LEAD THE CHARGE THE FASTER OUR COMPANIES—AND OUR WORLD— WILL MOVE FORWARD. STAND UP AND

LEAVE A LEGACY

I believe people can do anything they want, and hopefully, what they want is good for the planet. We each find ourselves at a capstone moment in our personal history. One day, we'll look back at this time and say we made an impact. At least, that's my hope for myself and for you. I want to look back and know we, together, had a positive effect on generations to come. This is a game we can all play. This can be our combined legacy.

This is ultimately the only thing that's real. We're lucky to have this place we call Planet Earth. It's where we live, and where future generations will thrive. The most profound legacy is, I believe, one that sustains this earth for future generations. There are a million ways to achieve that. You don't have to be an inventor; you can be part of a company that works toward a united legacy. However it looks, you should be contributing. You should be striving for cleaner air, cleaner water, safer environments, less violence, fewer chronic illnesses, more robust healthcare, and better quality of life.

This is what community is all about. We come together to achieve better, safer, more fulfilling environments. There is nothing more noble than taking action to contribute to your community in a lasting way. That is a legacy worthy of recognition.

A SENSE OF URGENCY

Bring a sense of urgency to the ideas you've learned in this book. Remember to look out from your bubble to the wider world. It's not enough to give your kids a good education and assume they'll be okay. We're all affected by the world at large, and it's on us to ensure it survives. If you're reading this book, you're in a privileged position to break free from the chains of "the normal way" and make a mark on the world. It's not just your duty to yourself and your children; it's the path to fulfillment. It's what will quiet the nagging feeling that you're wasting your time on this earth. Working for something bigger than yourself will set you free.

Keep in mind that you don't need to measure up to the mammoths of this world. We don't need more eccentric millionaires sending cars into space. The world will benefit most from smart, inspired people developing innovative ideas. Anyone can do that—even you. If that feels like a big ask, start with small steps. Yes, you want to aim big, but take small risks to strengthen your confidence. Wear red socks and work up from there.

Identify the impact you want to make on the world. You don't have to step outside your area of expertise. Solve macro problems in your industry by reimagining products and services, redesigning operations and supply chains, and aligning organizations into multidimensional sustainability. Whatever you choose, you'll find radical changes are radically fulfilling.

Then imagine how you'll create that change. Look for inspiration outside your day-to-day. Whiteboard ideas. Reimagine your industry. Anything is possible. Strengthen your resolve to innovate and your innovation skills by surrounding yourself with diversity of thought. It will help you avoid groupthink and set you up for more imaginative and fulfilling business leaps. Support that with an ecosystem of kindness. Remember: you don't need to be a jerk.

Stop waiting for permission to break free of the chains of expectation, and just do it already. Understand that no one else will push you on this. It has to come from you. Then, be inspired to take a leap and really reimagine your future. If you keep pushing forward, keep taking steps, and do it with a sense of urgency, you will leave a legacy to be proud of.

DREAM BIGGER

I go back to imagining my grandmother on the train in Belarus with nothing but the clothes on her back. Here I am, sitting in my comfortable home in New Orleans, and I can do anything—have anything—I want. My kid has a soccer game this afternoon. Maybe I'll have sushi after. Maybe I'll have a glass of wine while I scroll social media sites. This is not a difficult life. There's nothing as scary as standing in a new land with nothing. The worst thing I'll probably face in my lifetime is a personal health crisis. Thinking about my grandmother puts my own life in perspective. I realize I can have the same impact on my kids as she did on hers—even if it's in a very different way. I just need to dream bigger.

Whether you believe you're stuck, making progress, or

doing big things, you can always dream bigger. It's like sustainability. People say, "Well, we reduced our carbon footprint by 5 percent. We're sustainable now. We're done." You can never be done with sustainability. There's always more to improve upon. And you're never done with dreaming big. Whatever you're doing, you can reach further, make bigger leaps, and continually reimagine what's possible.

We need to do more. I hope I can inspire more companies to think like Truman's—to focus on disruption that simplifies products and services, to work all facets of an issue to make the world a better place. I hope I've inspired you to take action. To stop going through the fucking motions, floating through time like our presence has no impact on our earth. I mean, really, get off your ass. Stop looking at Facebook. Stop aimlessly surfing the internet. Realize that you're not some tiny elephant chained to a fencepost with no chance of moving anywhere. You're strong. You can break free, if you wish. Yank that fencepost from the ground, shake off the chains, and reimagine what your future could be. Dream big and make your mark on the world. I can't wait to see what you do.

ACKNOWLEDGMENTS

Thank you to Wade Forbes, who created the amazing illustrations for this book. It's a privilege to see these ideas brought to life this way.

Thank you to my wife, Marigny, whose work has always inspired me—and even inspired that goofy microwave button.

To my business partner, Alex, for taking a leap to make the world a little cleaner with Truman's.

To my kids, Evan and Will, for inspiring me to reimagine my future at work.

And to the thousands of people throughout history who broke free to make the world a better place.

ABOUT THE AUTHOR

JON BOSTOCK was a tethered elephant at General Electric for eleven years until he made his move and became the COO at Big Ass Fans (true story, real name). After restructuring the company and focusing on long-term economic sustainability, he was successful shepherding the company's landmark sale.

These concepts of disruption and sustainability inspired Jon to break free and start Truman's, a company designed to reduce waste and clutter in the consumer cleaning products industry.

Jon lives in New Orleans with his wife, Marigny, and their two children, Evan and Will.

CPSIA information can be obtained
at www.ICGtesting.com
Printed in the USA
LVHW090034180820
663477LV00007B/201/J